REMARKABLE

REMARKABLE

TOBY LAVIGNE

TABLE OF CONTENTS

DEDICATION 7
SPECIAL THANKS 9
   Special thought leaders 11
FOREWORD 13
THE REMARKABLE PROJECT 13
   by Dr. Stephen Franson 13
PREFACE 17
   Remarkable is Born 17
   It's just a breakfast 19
   Successful 21
   Greater than Success 23
INTRODUCTION 27
   Interpretation 27
FOUR - REMARKABLE TRANSITION 29
   Villain 29
   Hero 31
   Leaders 33
   The Age of Enlightenment 35
   Economic Agents 38
THREE - THE REMARKABLE FOUR 47
   Remarkable Element #1 -
   Fair Game 56
   Remarkable Element #2 -
   Inspiration 77
   Remarkable Element #3 –
   Tribal Platform 81

Remarkable Element #4 –
Alignment 89
Remarkable Recap 93

TWO - REMARKABLE STORIES 99
"Doc" Franson 103
"Captain" Karl of Lean Nation 110
"Bus Driver" Mark 122
"Coach" Glassman 132

ONE - YOUR REMARKABLE MISSION 145
Service Design 145
A Remarkable Rant 148
Remarkable Action 151

ENDNOTES 153

DEDICATION

To Emoo and her legacy;

i. Anything worth doing, is worth doing well

ii. Don't take yourself too seriously

iii. Be brave

iv. Remember, that sometimes, the greatest gift is letting others give to you.

My Dad for teaching me to serve

My girls – Shelly, Soleil, and Summer who inspire me every day

SPECIAL THANKS

All of my HubCast friends for believing in me and pushing me further **Amanda Vernor** – better late than never, the work we did helped make this happen and so did you **Amy Schnall** – the ultimate assistant **Doc Franson** – thanks for being in my corner **Dr. Christian** – your power is on **Brian Murphy** – a modern revolutionary and a heck of a chef **Bob Rosen** – exactly what I needed to hear, every time I needed to hear it **Captain Karl Wadensten** – thank you for your leadership and generosity **Chris Marsh** – steadfast and wise throughout, thank you **Darlene Hollywood** – your belief and support have been vital fuel **Dave Ianelli** – the only lawyer that has ever made me laugh **Frances Frei** – For sharing your wisdom and passion for Service Excellence and for supporting The Remarkable Project **Jim Coughlin** - Thank you for being you **Jody Underhill** – thanks for accelerating my learning curve and believing in TRP **Joe Baroni** for making room for my project and for being a great friend **Joey Diovisalvi** – the epitome of commitment **John Colosimo** – it's been a great journey so far, you know it better than most and your support has been invaluable. **John Cundiff** – An insanely great coach **Linda Kleinberg** – editor extraordinaire…thanks for pushing me **Mark Aesch** - for opening up the doors of the Rochester Genesee Regional Transit Authority and sharing one of the most remarkable turnarounds I've ever heard of **Marty Grothe** for pushing me to go do what I'm supposed to do, sorry I'm late **Matt Ortolani** – a stand up man among stand up men **Mr. John Berger** – kind and thoughtful soul **Portsmouth Crossfit, Jason Goulemas and Eric Morris** – for demonstrating 'tribe' **Rob, Annie, and Kate** – you're welcome **Remarkable Class 01 – Tomas Boiton, Andy Bugsby, Faith Jacobson, Noel Martinez, Matt Ortolani, Stephanie Waldrop,** – follow your intuition. **Sherra Sewell** – your enthusiasm is contagious **The HEYDAY Boys; Andy Bugsby, Rob Evans** – never stop taking risks to make PBC weird **Dan Sullivan and all my friends at The Strategic Coach** – for demonstrating the power of getting out of your backyard to build a bigger future **Tim Vogel** – for kicking me in the butt to publish this book already! **My Remarkable Unum Mates; Andy Katz, Bret Morrison, Dave Barlow, Dave McCue, Dick Simon, Don Smith, Harley Frank, Jamie Cornell, Jim Kellogg** – 0% agenda, 100% heart **Carl Youngman** – incredible and timely moral support - **YPO** for opening me up to the remarkable world **Zahra Kanji** – you have a remarkable future ahead of you.

SPECIAL THOUGHT LEADERS

Every teacher stands on the shoulders of the giants before them. These remarkable teachers have each influenced and enhanced my own thinking about the changes that are taking place in our economy today, the challenges we face as organizations, leaders and individuals, and the strategies to become the best leaders and individuals we can possibly become. I am grateful for each of you;

- Clayton Christianson
- Steven Covey
- John Cundiff
- Dr. John Demartini
- Frances Frei
- Seth Godin
- Dan Pink
- Steven Pressfield
- Sir Ken Robinson
- Stan Slap
- Coach Greg Glassman

FOREWORD
THE REMARKABLE PROJECT

BY DR. STEPHEN FRANSON

I have spent the last 15 years taking care of patients who simply wanted to get healthier. They have presented with a multitude of symptoms, crises and problems – but ultimately, they all just wanted to get well again.

These people have most likely exhausted the traditional healthcare system that favors treating symptoms or pain solving. This approach will often temporarily quiet a symptom, but usually just kicks the problem down the road. The patient typically experiences what we call "up and down on the way down".

Not only is this ineffective in achieving the ultimate goal (getting well) but it is unsustainable; devouring resources

- and tragically, the patient misses out on what is possible: an extraordinary life.

The Wellness Paradigm dictates an entirely different approach to achieving the ultimate goal. This perspective on health drives an entirely new set of questions.

I start every new patient relationship with 2 simple, yet profound questions:

1. Are you as healthy as you want to be?

2. What do you need to start doing to get there?

The Wellness Paradigm holds that we are designed to be healthy. In fact, for about 99.6% of us, our genes are perfectly hard-wired to create health. If we regularly give the body what it innately requires and avoid those things that are innately toxic; we will express health. The *expression* of health is our default.

Conversely, if we are not expressing health – or we are "sick"; it simply means that something is *interfering* with the expression of health.

Two things cause this interference:

1. Deficiency

2. Toxicity

Ultimately your health is largely determined by the lifestyle choices that you repeatedly make. This leads to a clear conclusion: **"You don't get sick, you are sick."**

In this Information Age, there is no shortage of research or information to support this truth. We have never had the level of access to good information about how to get healthy and stay healthy as we enjoy today, yet we have never been sicker. The bottom line is that people don't need more information, they need transformation.

Toby LaVigne believes that the same can be said for the state of business today.

The current condition of the business world is the perfect analog to the sickness burden that we face in Healthcare. The state of the marketplace resembles the floor of hospital filled with the consequences of a broken model. **Toby boldly suggests that the natural state of a business doing worthwhile work is growth and engagement.** Remarkable makes a compelling case for the Wellness Paradigm as the savior of the modern business.

LaVigne debunks the traditional Management Model of treating symptoms and pain solving. He proposes an alternative to the outdated practices of the traditional management and self development.

He proposes that we will never realize our potential if we continue to kick our problems down the road and suggests that we set our sights on becoming extraordinary – remarkable even.

In short, LaVigne champions one over-riding narrative: **You don't get remarkable, you are remarkable.**

Toby unapologetically calls us all to "remarkability" – not for the sake of being remarkable in itself, but rather for the profound positive effect that ripples out from the center of a remarkable organization.

In this book Ultimately, Toby asks you the two most important questions:

1. Are you as remarkable as you want to be?

2. What do you need to start doing to get there?

S Franson

PREFACE

The old economy is out and the new one arrived while we were trying to figure out the Internet. Navigating this new world is proving difficult, but it's to be expected. After all, we were trained for the old one, and few of us actually foresaw the profound changes in human motivation or the massive capability of the Internet.

REMARKABLE IS BORN

Remarkable is the new success. This book is about the profound difference between success and remarkability, it's about creating more value with less effort, and it's about how remarkable business can elevate the human experience.

Perhaps like you, I've been a long-term student of 'success'. I've read, and studied and practiced the habits of the most successful people I could find. But even as

I racked up accomplishments, true satisfaction seemed fleeting.

Slowly I began to question much of what I was taught about success and whether I had my ladder against the right wall. I came to notice that the people I admired most were great for reasons that were more profound than goal achievement; there was something more going on. They were having much more fun than the successful people I knew.

They were working hard for sure, but there was certainly a sense of flow. It seemed like the congruence between who they were and what they did was perfect.

It seemed like the harder they worked, the more support they received. Opportunities seemed to naturally appear for them. Their energy seemed limitless.

And it hit me, these people are remarkable! They get noticed more and talked about more, not just because of their results, but because of the sense of congruence we witness between who they are and the difference they make in this world.

People simply want to be around them and to lend support to whatever they are working on, if only to experience a glimpse of what it is to be like them. They were more 'successful' *because* they were remarkable.

*No problem can be solved from the same level of
consciousness that created it.*

- Albert Einstein

IT'S JUST A BREAKFAST

We are having breakfast at the Round a Bout Diner next to the Portsmouth, NH traffic circle. My wife Shelly and my good friend Dr. Stephen Franson are taking turns grabbing bites and energetically discussing our shared and intense interest in health, nutrition and Crossfit. On this particular occasion we met to discuss our daughter Soleil who has really swollen tonsils, which are hindering the quality of her sleep, and ours. Ok, mostly Shelly's.

Soleil's doctor had recommended that she have her tonsils and adenoids removed. "It's no big deal," she said, "She has over 500 other lymph nodes in her body, she won't even miss them." This didn't sit well with us. If they weren't necessary, why do we have them? And why were they swollen to begin with? Shouldn't we figure that out first before doing surgery to permanently remove body parts from a four year old?!

So we ask Stephen, "There is all sorts of information on the web about tonsils and adenoids and strep throat and surgery. We can't find any information on what makes them swell to begin with. How can we go through with a surgery if we don't even know what's wrong?"

Stephen gives us a knowing smile that confirms how important our question is. "The body's natural state is to express health. If the body is not healthy there are really only three things it can be; a deficiency of some kind, a toxin, or both. In other words something is missing, or something is there that shouldn't be, or both."

"Something is missing, or something is there that shouldn't be, or both"

Now, I tend to think a lot about what makes things tick. I am always trying to connect the seemingly unrelated and looking for natural patterns. I believe that there is a root cause to everything and despise symptomatic approaches to problem solving. I simply don't believe that treating symptoms is sustainable, effective or efficient.

My mind began to wander as I reflected on what Stephen had just said; "Something is missing or something is there that shouldn't be, or both".

I'm thinking about how this ties to another intense interest - business and life design and my concept for the Remarkable Project. I was on a mission to find a better method to navigate business and life. Our economy and society are living breathing organisms subject to the same natural laws as our bodies. The symptoms we are experiencing economically, physically, and fiscally are not a result of deficiencies in government programs, laws and regulations; the root cause goes much deeper than that. The solution is sustainable, much simpler, much healthier.

SUCCESSFUL

I leap to thinking about Soleil's doctor. She is a very bright, friendly doctor. She went to a top school and got excellent grades. You could easily describe her as "successful". As in, "she has a successful Ear, Nose and Throat practice". How many times have you heard of someone described as being "successful"? "I hear he has quite a successful business." You get the idea.

Excuse me, but what the hell does "successful" mean? Does it mean that they achieved *their* goals? *Our* goals? Which goals? Is it because of their title? Their earnings? Their house? Their car? The school they went to?

Back to our doctor. If you are a parent reading this, then you will clearly appreciate our mindset that success as it related to our daughter was getting to the bottom of the tonsil issue – finding the root cause and treating it versus just getting rid of symptoms. Somehow I didn't get the feeling that our definition of success and the doctor's were the same.

What I observed was a well-regarded doctor who looked at our daughter in a chair for less than 10 minutes and on the spot recommended surgery that represented over $2,000 in revenue, a substantial risk to our daughter, and unknown long-term consequences.

I don't mean to say that she is corrupt or unethical. But let's be real, the surgeon paradigm defines success not by eliminating the need for surgeries, but rather by performing them well and often. You have a symptom, they have a surgical solution. We were talking with our friend Dr. Stephen precisely because he is a wellness doctor. He defines 'success' in terms of discovering the origin of the symptom and remedying the cause. By Doc's paradigm, the fewer surgeries and pills the better.

> *For those who are curious: We followed Dr. Stephen's approach and looked harder at eliminating toxins. We follow the Paleo diet, which avoids processed foods and dairy. Soleil's diet was already very low in gluten and dairy, but not 100%. We took it to 100% and guess what, the swelling reduced and the snoring is gone. No surgery, better sleep, happier kid, happier Mom and Dad. Remarkable results.*

This paradigm misalignment between customer and service provider objectives is present not just in health care, but also in the creation and delivery of countless products and services everywhere.

The 'symptom management' paradigm is pervasive in our society and I can trace it back to the overwhelming majority of our social, business, and personal struggles.

The natural byproduct of this myopic approach is dissatisfied customers, unhappy employees, government regulation, distrust, and a whole pile of other harmful side effects that are making us sick, figuratively and literally.

If you want to understand why our health, wealth and morale have been declining sharply, you need look no further than the success paradigm and the tools for achieving 'success'.

GREATER THAN SUCCESS

This book is a call to join the Remarkable Revolution. It lays bare the conflict of our time; the struggle to overcome a century of education, and 'proven' management habits.

No matter how it is disguised, the core struggle of this time is the choice between temporary success and it's toxic after effects or lasting remarkability with positive side benefits. It's about the urgent need to redefine success. It's for you and about you. It's about what you have the potential to become.

I am going to urge and inspire you to take a hard look at the tactics and strategies you have been taught to use to pursue success and how you can tweak them to live life on your terms and 'stand out' in a very big way.

Whether you are an individual trying to advance your career or a business owner trying to grow your business, separating yourself from the pack is vital.

If you don't stand out, if you don't stand for something remarkable, then increasingly, you will not be trusted and you won't matter. And 'not mattering' threatens your wealth, your health, and your spirit. In fact, I can trace nearly every problem we face individually and as a society to 'not mattering', or as you will soon see, disengagement.

But there is one really big problem that every individual and business now faces; the strategies and tactics that got us where we are today cannot take us where we need to go next.

The reason is that the 'tried and true' tactics of standing out are no longer effective. There is so much 'noise' in the world today. So many offers, calls, messages, promises, requests, claims, and stuff that clutter up the airwaves. This noise is not only higher in quantity; it is also lower in quality. There are so many half-truths and manipulations being thrown at us, that we are all becoming somewhat numb and increasingly adept at tuning out the noise all together – if only out of necessity.

Only the truly remarkable seem to garner sustainable attention.

Paradoxically, our *need* to stand out is increasing right along with the noise factor. The methods we were taught to pursue 'success' are failing to sustainably differentiate our business careers or us.

It is time to reach for something much greater than success.

"What?!" you say, "What's greater than success?"

I want to inspire you to become REMARKABLE!

> **Remarkable:** a person who has **cleverly infused** their **mission** into their **career** and created a **loyal following** by delivering **massive value** through **focused service and life design**.

Here's a simple truth. People love to be around remarkable people. Remarkable people benefit from a tailwind of support that successful people do not. Remarkable people and businesses literally ride *with* a certain flow. The strategic decision to pursue remarkability makes your business and your life run more smoothly.

We'll talk much more about the elements of remarkable. For now, just know that the decision to become remarkable can deliver more than you can possibly imagine.

INTRODUCTION

INTERPRETATION

As you read this book I am going to challenge you to think seriously about the personal and professional consequences of tapping into a 'bigger why', a bigger reason to do what you do. Not from a belly button staring perspective, but from a warm blooded "I want to kick some serious butt in this lifetime" perspective.

This is a book about getting BIG results. It's about becoming someone that people greatly admire and talk about in ways that 'success' simply cannot match. And it is also about how to not get left behind.

Most conversations about 'finding purpose' include clichés and somehow suggest that your 'true self' should be an artist, musician, writer, etc. There's an assumption that you must change your vocation in order to 'find yourself'. I'm not suggesting that. In fact, for almost everyone, your best chance to be Remarkable is to build on the business or career that you already have.

So as you are reading, keep an open mind. You will see some examples which I believe will amaze you and inspire you to imagine applications for The Remarkable Method in any industry and by any type of leader. Your existing business or career is a platform for the expression of your unique formula. That expression will yield you greater results and satisfaction than you could possibly imagine.

My favorite part about remarkability is that it is attainable and possible for everyone. There are as many paths to being remarkable as there people on this planet. Everyone *can be* remarkable. Everyone *is meant to be remarkable.* Everyone *needs* to be remarkable.

FOUR
REMARKABLE TRANSITION

VILLAIN

There are a thousand hacking at the branches of evil to one who is striking at the root.
-Henry David Thoreau

75% of our workforce reports being disengaged from their work. Seventy five percent! Nearly 8 out of every 10 people you come across are unhappy with their career. They dread the thought of going to work during their commute, they don't like being there while they're at work, they're drained when they get home, and go to great lengths to forget about it.

Disengagement. It's such a clinical sounding word. It doesn't elicit a lot of emotion. But think about it for a moment. Being engaged is what life is all about. Learning, growing, being interested, curious, challenged, and sometimes…victorious. As a leader, you already know what that feels like, but perhaps you haven't realized how little of this most people experience.

So what?

The problem with disengagement is that disengaged people become disillusioned. They begin to think that there is no hope, that there is no place for them, and that perhaps the 'system' must be broken. Disillusioned people become increasingly unhappy at home and at work.

And unhappy people who don't see a light at the end of the tunnel adopt a victim mentality. They become fertile ground for messengers that promise institutionalized solutions. They want relief and they want it now.

This is the defining conversation in politics today. There is a tremendous conflict between the engaged and the disengaged that is deteriorating into class warfare.

Entrepreneurial-minded people like you believe that you can construct your own reality. It's more than just being optimistic; it's about a sense of who you are, what you can do, and finding a way to make a difference.

This mindset may be second nature to you, but to over 75% of our population, it is not. And that other 75% is influencing social policy around the world in ways that threaten not only your ability to be entrepreneurial, but that threaten the freedom and quality of life for EVERYONE.

Freedom and quality of life are fighting words to entrepreneurs. Your very worldview is that you have the power to create more freedom and increase your quality of life. To you it's not just a belief, it's a RIGHT!

That RIGHT is being threatened, and we must do something about it.

HERO

The hero is the person who leverages who he or she is and what he or she knows to such a degree and in such a personal way that they engage ever-greater numbers of their teams, their customers and their communities.

They create a work environment that increases engagement, and they aspire to something far greater than success. The hero aspires to become remarkable.

Heroes are people like you who care about themselves, their legacies, and the people that they impact. They overcome social patterning and business norms to achieve success. The heroes are people like you who refuse to accept that disengagement is an acceptable outcome… for anyone.

This book is about how you can become a hero and help rescue personal freedom and quality of life from the jaws of disengagement.

To do it we're going to have to redefine success and commit our enterprises to become powerful social levers of change, freedom, and fulfillment. Not just for you, but for all of the people you impact.

And just in case you're starting to fear that I am proposing some sort of anti capitalistic business 'love in'. Not to worry. I believe that profits are the catalyst of remarkability. Profitability and remarkability are highly correlated. My strategy is to increase profits by increasing engagement, the side benefits of which will change your life by epic proportions.

My strategy not only increases engagement, it dramatically increases your differentiation. And as you know, differentiation is business code for higher margins, lower customer acquisition costs, greater customer loyalty, even higher employee retention, and much more.

My vision is to engage the greatest social change levers that exist, business leaders like you. My Remarkable strategy is to rally already successful people like you and to challenge and support you to pursue the journey of becoming more and more remarkable.

By enlisting a legion of entrepreneurs, we will increase engagement, freedom, and quality of life. More engaged people, fewer victims. Fewer victims…fewer supporters of institutionalized solutions, AND more examples and proof that business can and should be the social program of choice.

LEADERS

Why do some people manage to break free from the rules they were taught in school while others do not? It's a tricky question. Nearly all of my friends are entrepreneurs and, one way or another, most of us discovered two really important things early in our lives. The first is that we wanted to take control of our destinies. The second was that we could!

My life as an entrepreneur started with the desire to solve a problem that would earn me some money and create some financial independence.

When I was much younger, I noticed that there were two problems with how snow was removed from the driveways in our New England neighborhood. The first was that the plows usually didn't arrive until after the homeowner's normal work departure time, and the second was that the plows couldn't get close enough to the garage doors or clear the walkways and stairs.

So I created a sales flyer for our neighbors promising a clear driveway before they left for work and I included clearing their walks and stairs up to their doors. My brother Rob and I developed a two-person plow that we would run behind to clear the driveway. Often this required us to make several overnight visits to keep up with larger storms.

One day my best customer, Mr. Savickas, who was also an encouraging fan, told me that I was an **entrepreneur**. I think it was the first time I ever heard the word, but I fell in love with it immediately. I loved business, but **entrepreneurship** sounded even cooler, and I suddenly realized that I didn't have to 'fit in' to be successful. In fact, the path to success actually *rewards* stepping outside the norm.

There was a word for who I was, and it sounded like a good thing?! In one moment I got a real world identity and a compliment that was an important early spark that shaped my view of what was possible.

Ok, so what about the other 75%? Why do they see themselves as pawns instead of kings?

THE AGE OF ENLIGHTENMENT

The paradigm through which most of us filter our world, most of the time, was given to us in our early years of education. The way that *we think* about what we do to become successful, how *we organize* what we do to become successful, and how *we actually act* to become successful come from our earliest introduction to life and work. They come in large part from our experiences at school.

School as we know it today was fashioned in a much different time (The Age of Enlightenment) and under vastly different circumstances (The Industrial Revolution) than today.

As you might imagine, there were some inherent assumptions at work; beliefs that we had about intelligence, the work that we expected our children to perform throughout their careers, and the way that we thought about the potential of people.

At the time, intelligence was thought to be academic; knowledge of the classics and deductive reasoning were the key concepts to master. Our thoughts of work were shaped by the factory assembly line. And there was a belief that not everyone was capable of learning. In fact, many people in power thought that only an elite few were capable of academic excellence.

LIMITED VIEW OF INTELLIGENCE

Not surprisingly, there were and continue to be consequences to these design criteria. First, we emphasized one form of intelligence. That singular emphasis shaped the model most of us experienced; the accumulation of knowledge through memorization. Historically, society placed a great value on being able to supply rote information and follow rules.

So, naturally there was a great emphasis in our education system to memorize information, to test our recollection, and to conform. Yet today, information access is not scarce. Today we place a higher value on being able to organize information and provide access to it rather than actually possessing it. With that in mind, let's remember that the greatest creations have always been and will always be significant departures from the established ways of doing things.

ASSEMBLY LINE LEARNING

The industrial revolution was all about manipulating objects and economies of scale. So this thinking naturally went into education design in the form of standardized curricula delivered to students in batches as if being sent down an assembly line. If the delivery didn't match your learning style, you were probably out of luck.

ACADEMIC ELITE

Our limited beliefs about human potential and intelligence produced the idea that there were basically two types of people (and two types of jobs); smart, "academic" or not smart "non academic".

One unfortunate consequence of this is that our approach to education has favored one type of intelligence and alienated the rest along the way. As a result, the vast majority of human beings go through life without knowing or exploring their potential.

DISENGAGEMENT!

It is also true that the vast majority of businesses operate without knowing or exploring the potential of their teams.

ECONOMIC AGENTS

I can't think of a better term to describe the prevailing business attitude toward employees; economic agents. You can just see how it is an extension of the factory and education worldview. Employees are simply inputs in the system, not humans with goals, and values and dreams, and talents, but economic agents.

Where did this view come from?

We've all heard that our greatest human need is to survive. You may also have learned that we seek rewards and avoid punishment. We're animals, too, after all.

Dan Pink, author of Drive, calls these motivations 1.0 and 2.0. Motivation 1.0; seek food, clothing and shelter. Motivation 2.0; seek carrots, avoid sticks. In his book Dan does a brilliant job outlining the case and the research where this is true, but even more importantly, and astonishingly, where it is NOT TRUE.

It turns out that carrot and stick like incentives work very well *only* for rudimentary tasks.

When I was a kid one of my summer jobs was working on a 'head boat' that took tourists deep sea fishing two times a day. We got paid $8 per half-day trip to cut bait, net fish, haul anchor, and on those inevitable windy days, tend to green passengers. The job was highly sought after by boys in our town. "Why?" you rightly ask. It was partly for the 'cool' factor of working on the ocean every day (intrinsic motivation), but also because we had the opportunity to earn some really excellent bonuses and tips (extrinsic motivation).

The passengers were typically visiting tourists who either couldn't or didn't want to clean their own fish. To earn extra cash, we filleted fish for a quarter-a-piece plus tips on the trip back to the harbor. With many hundreds of fish on board and a limited amount of time to get back to the harbor, we were well motivated to work quickly.

I have vivid memories of racing my fellow deck hands to see who could clean the most fish. No one had to manage or motivate us. We knew the job and we knew that the relationship between what we produced and our financial reward was crystal clear. The carrot worked perfectly.

BAD CARROT

Contrast the fish-cleaning example with much of the work that needs doing today. Labor costs in this country and other developed nations have resulted in the vast majority of manual and rudimentary jobs like fish cleaning to be sent overseas where labor is cheap and readily available.

Think about it. Think about your own service experiences - in nearly every case, you expect the person behind the desk or on the phone to be able to think for himself or herself - at least to some degree. You likely expect this of your employees and colleagues, as well.

Yet you still experience people on your own team and on the teams of others who can't or won't think creatively to solve problems – even those problems that only require a small amount of basic creativity. And no combination of, incentives, compensation programs, call monitoring, surveys, policies, or procedures seems to result in great service.

CARROT RESEARCH

The research that Dan Pink, author of Drive, cites regarding extrinsic motivations - Carrots and Sticks - clearly shows when these motivators work and - more importantly for you- when they don't. Here is an excerpt from Drive that really hits home;

"We humans respond to rewards when they are awarded for completing simple tasks. When rewards are applied to tasks requiring even a minor amount of creativity and complexity, they serve to DECREASE output! Why?"

WORK AND PLAY

Rewards can actually signal that a task is undesirable. If you have children then you have firsthand experience with this. You can get kids to pick up rocks by making it a rock collection game and they will do it with glee and for free. Tell your kid that you'll pay them to do it, and they may still do it, but it won't be fun, and you likely will struggle to get them to do it for free in the future.

One summer when my siblings and I were young, my mother created a 'chores game'. She posted a score sheet on the fridge where our point totals were recorded. For each chore we performed, she awarded us a certain number of points. I can still remember mowing our rather large lawn and earning 9 points for the two hour effort.

We had been pestering my mother all summer to find out what our 'points' were worth. I was the oldest, so naturally I was leading the point race in late August. I remember a feeling of pride and accomplishment in seeing proof of my contributions add up.

We were all anxious to learn what our 'points' meant. Notice that I said, 'meant', not worth. We wanted to know what our efforts stood for, we wanted them to be meaningful.

Finally in late August my Mom relented and declared the points worth one penny each. One penny! Mowing the lawn was worth 9 cents for two hours work! We've had inflation since then, but I'm not that old. People on deserted islands were earning more than 4 ½ cents per hour!

All summer long we were performing chores and earning points for the fun of it. It really didn't matter what a point was worth, it was just satisfying to see our totals increase. The chore point game died an instant death the moment we learned that points were money. And honestly, it really wouldn't have mattered how much a point was worth, the emotional result would have been similar.

To my Mom's credit, I think that she intuitively knew what the result would be, but she gave into conventional thinking. Fortunately for us, she has been a role model for resisting peer pressure. "If everyone else was going to jump off a bridge, would you want to do that, too?"

Knowing what I know now, one great approach would have been to simply say that we are going to have a points celebration dinner. We're all going out to a restaurant, you can order what you want and we'll just celebrate a great summer and all of your hard work. I guarantee that we would have been eager for the points to be reset after that dinner and to run the game again through Christmas.

Hmmm. Note to self – create chores point game for our girls.

I THOUGHT WE WERE FRIENDS

Carrots and sticks, or 'if then' rewards create a contingent dynamic in the relationship. They infer a lack of trust. "I assume that you won't do a good job, so I'll bribe you either with a reward or coerce you with a punishment."

Studies prove that motivation is everything, but you don't need a study to prove this concept, you've experienced it throughout your entire life.

When you were in school, was your focus and the focus of your classmates on the love and journey of learning for learning's sake, or just to get good grades? Did anyone cheat on tests? Do you know anyone that never cheated, in any way, during their whole time in school? How many students do you know who picked up those required reading books and read them in their free time? How about during the summer after the school year or even many years later, did *you* pick those books back up again?

You're reading this book because you want to, because you are curious to learn how to accomplish more with less. It's about autonomy. When you get to decide the "why" of learning and doing, when you do things for strong internally driven reasons… it just feels good. But when the 'if then' contingent dynamic is brought back into play, it ceases to be our choice, it ceases to be enjoyable, sustaining it is virtually impossible.

We often hear that business is about people. "Our greatest asset is our people". That sounds great and of course it's true. But now that you understand the limits of if-then rewards, what do you think happens when an organization or business uses them? Do their greatest assets feel valued and important? Do they go the extra mile? Do they feel engaged?

The answer, of course, is no. They feel like objects, like economic agents, and eventually they begin to act like them, too. When our survival needs are basically met, humans will only go the extra mile for *intrinsic* reasons. We spend time on our hobbies for free - because it feels good to challenge ourselves and grow, and it supports our deepest values.

> *"A raise is only a raise for thirty days; after that, it's just your salary."*
> – DAVID RUSSO, VP OF HUMAN RESOURCES AT SAS INSTITUTE

7 DRAWBACKS TO CARROTS AND STICKS[1]

1. They extinguish intrinsic motivation

2. They diminish true performance

3. They crush creativity

4. They crowd out best behavior

5. They encourage shortcuts, cheating, and unethical behavior

6. They become addictive

7. They foster short-term thinking

THREE
THE REMARKABLE FOUR

Ok, so most people are disengaged because they don't feel valued. And business tries to *re-engage* them using carrots and sticks, but that doesn't work because they lack a personal reason for going the extra mile.

THE fundamental issue we are facing today is a profound shift in the primary source of human motivation. The last economy thrived by satisfying the human need to improve our standard of living. The factory economy brought us out of the woods literally and figuratively. It brought us mass access to electricity, heat, clothing, transportation and communication.

And now that our survival needs have been met, we are shifting into a higher motivational gear. The new economy requires that we lead with an emphasis on satisfying *intrinsic* reasons for doing work.

Perhaps you've taken your personal motivation for granted. Let's take a look at what people really, really *want and need* to feel engaged.

They need four things;

1. A game they can win (most of the time)

2. Inspiration

3. Belonging

4. Alignment

We're going to take a deeper look at all four but first let me introduce each of them briefly.

FAIR GAME

You can scarcely read or watch an advertisement claim today without finding yet another example of marketing promising more than operations can deliver. It's discouraging and frustrating but its common practice. There is growing evidence that an increasingly skeptical consumer audience is becoming more and more immune to this tactic.

The problem of course is that eventually the prospect discovers that the advertising claim doesn't live up to the real service experience, and then they end up disappointed at a minimum and possibly downright hostile. And here is where the problems begin.

What does this do to the front line inside the business? Do they take a deep breath, grin, bear it, and forget it never happened, again and again and again? Does their engagement deepen or do they begin to develop a hardened shell to distance themselves in self-defense? The answer of course is obvious, and it's one of several conditions that contribute to the epidemic statistic that 75% of the population is disengaged at work.

Everyone enjoys a challenge, but we all need the reward of winning, or the game eventually becomes not worth playing. We all need to believe that we have a fighting chance.

INSPIRATION

We all seek to fulfill our highest personal values. When we participate in activities that feed our hunger to fulfill our personal values, we become intrinsically motivated.

As I've already mentioned, the prevailing management mindset and reaction is to attempt to 'inspire' teams using extrinsic techniques; Raises, bonuses, incentives, slogans, team events, training, reviews, agreements, contracts… the list goes on an on.

As O'Reilly III and Pfeffer, authors of Hidden Value pointed out,

> *"Management's job is to design ever more sophisticated control and incentive systems to ensure that the necessary teamwork occurs."*

There is no shortage of managers focused more on treating symptoms than addressing root causes. So disengagement has been on the rise; it's become an epidemic. As a consequence, our entrepreneurial way of life is being threatened. Business is being blamed for our society's woes and they're coming after us with pitchforks and torches.

I'm betting that when you see evidence of this in the news you feel that *your* values are being threatened. One of the best ways to tell if something is important to you is to feel it being taken away. We're going to look at how to tap the incredibly powerful force of values and mission on an organization-wide scale.

BELONGING

We are tribal, not just emotionally, but biologically. It is in our programming to belong. Biologically we are programmed to belong to survive. If you go back far enough, we needed to collaborate to build shelters, collect food, raise our young and fight off predators.

Getting expelled from the group meant certain death. So learning to 'fit in' is a pretty powerful urge. It may sound primitive, but we ALL want to belong.

Everyone we lead wants to belong. Just look at the lengths people will go to just to belong; updating their Facebook status, being a sports fan, tattoos, fashion, drugs, getting into a certain school, and on and on. Transforming your business from a place to work into a place to belong is a tremendously powerful advantage that will greatly diminish a large portion of the 'management' challenges that most business leaders face. I will dig into this soon.

As a part of their membership everyone wants to feel important. We all want to experience the thrill of getting really, really great at something and playing a role on a team that truly values our contributions. At the moment our daughters are ages 3 and 4, and I am reminded daily of the power of feeling valued.

Our girls are constantly asking my wife, Shelly, and me if they can help with something. They get a huge charge out of helping pour an ingredient in a recipe or helping me hold a drill to fasten something into the wall.

Everyone, and I mean everyone, wants to feel like they play an important role in their tribe. Yet the prevailing management mindset is to require people to act like machines that are programmed to follow processes 'by the book', and then struggle with their team's seeming inability to *'think'* for themselves. Is it any wonder that customer service and disengagement are both out of control?

If you tell an entrepreneur that they have to stay on script, if you ignore their input, and you attempt to 'lead' them with carrots and sticks you will be missing out on their best stuff, they'll tune out and eventually leave.

Now, Perhaps not everyone is as committed as you, but don't confuse the fact that they stay physically with the fact that they don't have to stay emotionally. Businesses measure absenteeism, but those statistics pale in comparison to actual levels of *presenteeism*. Everyone has some of their own 'best stuff' to offer, yet the prevailing approach to business by even some of the best intentioned business owners and managers systematically snuffs it out.

We all want to go to work to contribute and grow and become great at something – and we want to do it to a level where we are genuinely recognized and valued for what we bring to the team. This is called mastery and we'll be looking at how to tap into this, as well.

ALIGNMENT

Remarkable people and businesses are aligned. Their service is their purpose and their purpose is their service. They stay true to their area of focus and their inspired reason for focusing on it. In remarkable leaders you will find highly integrated character. They eat, sleep and drink their purpose. They have exceptional integrity.

Typically when we talk about integrity we hear values like honesty come up. I often hear people say that integrity is doing the right thing even when no one is looking. But what is the 'right thing'? I want everyone who reads this book to consider a different approach to integrity.

Being remarkable isn't about being liked by everyone or even about being morally correct in the eyes of others. It is about consistency of purpose, it's about a powerful offer that addresses the needs of a specific community. Whether or not YOU particularly like or approve of someone who fits this description, you must recognize that they are remarkable and that they have amassed a loyal following.

A big part of the struggle for businesses and individuals is that they compromise their integrity. They sell something they don't really believe in or they work with a customer that doesn't really fit, or keep an employee that isn't working out. While these choices are often defended as pragmatic and necessary, it is still important to recognize that they are also "ANTI REMARKABLE".

Consistent alignment between our service and our intention is essential to remarkability.

YOU'VE ALREADY AT LEAST DABBLED IN REMARKABILITY

As a leader, you learned long ago to create your own game, a game that gave you a fighting chance to live life on your terms. You probably followed some internal dreams that have been a source of inspiration to you, you have continuously challenged yourself, and you enjoy the satisfaction of growth and achievement.

Whether you have been conscious of it or not, you have probably been pursuing a path toward becoming remarkable. My questions to you are these;

1. What would happen if you took these four elements and wove them into your business model in a larger and possibly more conscious way?

2. What would happen to your team's engagement level?

3. What would happen to your engagement level?

4. How would that impact your customers?

5. What management challenges would diminish as a result?

6. What would your employees tell their friends and family about how business really is and really can be?

7. And how would all of this impact the quality of life within your sphere of influence?

8. What message would you and your organization be sending about the social contribution of business?

REMARKABLE ELEMENT #1 - FAIR GAME

I first met the developer of the Service Excellence Design model, Harvard Professor Frances Frei, when I was creating my last company, HubCast. After reading her article, The Four Things a Service Business Must Get Right, I instantly fell in love with the simplicity and profound impact of her model and contacted her to help us.

Frances turned out to be as friendly and helpful as she is brilliant, and her support and the support of her outstanding MBA student Zahra Kanji turned out to be invaluable in designing our award-winning service model.

HAPPY

Service Excellence is often confused with attempting to 'make the customer happy." Trying to make anyone or everyone happy is an impossible job. It's so easy for the efforts to backfire and create ill will vs. good will. It's generally easy to copy and, in the end, it's not satisfying.

When a hotel has a service failure they sometimes try to throw perks and goodies at the customer in an attempt to make them happy; a free drink or a room upgrade or whatever. The perks are usually only provided once you have complained, and have the feel of a page out of a playbook called: "How to shut up an angry customer."

The path to making a customer happy is to deeply satisfy them to begin with, and then let the happiness manifest as a result of the good experience. Remarkable Service Design can deeply satisfy your customers on a consistent basis because:

1. Your employees will be operating within a service design that consistently works. This saves tremendous energy reserves for attitude to deal with exceptions in a personal way.

2. Your customers will be interacting with a service that is consistently reliable. This differentiates your company, increases loyalty, and adds many more good things to the health of your business.

SERVICE DESIGN

I am going to share a model with you now that can have a very profound effect on your organization. There are four parts to remarkability; I'm going to begin with service design.

My friend Frances Frei had an opportunity to work with senior management in a large international bank. Their primary complaint was that no matter how the incentives or training programs were changed, the branch-level customer experience did not improve.

Frances suggested that senior management spend time working at a branch. After a single day on the frontline, a manager reported back:

"From the time the doors opened, customers were yelling at me... and by the end of the day, I was yelling back."

A large component of the poor service we experience is due to poor service design. The lack of customer focus and bad attitudes we regularly encounter develop from frustration which, in a management mindset environment, leads to more rules and control which only serve to create more frustration and negative feelings.

A senior manager, spending one day on the frontline, should be able to control her cool for at least one day, right? But she couldn't stomach it for even one day.

Why?

Because the service design set her and the rest of the branch workers (and the customers) up for failure. It was simply not possible for the service operation to meet the expectations set by marketing.

As managers we easily overlook the unintended consequences of our decisions over time – especially those that seem insignificant or small at the time. We can fail to consider the larger, longer-term impacts of the many decisions we make to deal with a variety of new product, service and customer events. The bottom line is that great service is more than employees with good attitudes willing to 'go the extra mile' for their customers. It requires great service design. In short, our teams need to have a fighting chance.

WHAT HAPPENED TO GOOD OLD FASHIONED SERVICE?

It is so easy to say things like, "People have such lousy attitudes these days". "No one cares like they used to". "Whatever happened to good old fashioned service?"

The answer is that the world got complicated and that an assembly line mentality isn't equipped to handle the new realities of business. In fact, it's exacerbating it. That's why it's time for a new approach. That approach is your ticket to greatness. Remarkability.

You can attempt to alter your hiring practices so that you only select those candidates with great attitudes, but even sunshiny people can get beat down over time. If you want an employee to deliver great service on a consistent basis, then they need to believe that they are playing a game they can win.

DEFINE YOUR REMARKABLE TERRITORY

Let's take a look at the air travel industry. . Southwest Airlines has had the best performance, by nearly every measure, of any of the airlines, yet it is famous for being the least luxurious. Why is that?

Southwest claims its 'remarkable territory' is low fares and friendly service, and they are unapologetic about all of the amenities they don't provide such as assigned seating, in-flight meals, fancy airport lounges, or a first class cabin.

The reason Southwest has a loyal following is that, by and large, passengers get what they expect. By disciplining themselves to focus on their 'remarkable territory' – low fairs and friendly service - Southwest plays a game it can win. Southwest knows that trying to be too many things to too many people is the path to mediocrity. 'Jack of all trades, master of none" is a race to the bottom.

FUNDING YOUR REMARKABLE TERRITORY

Being great at something is not cheap, so in order to earn a profit we have to find creative ways to pay for it. Let's look at how Southwest is able to offer lower fares than any other airline and be the ONLY airline with long-term profitability. There have been periods of time that

Southwest's profitability has exceeded all of the other US Airlines COMBINED!

DA PLANES

Southwest operates a limited set of aircraft. Limiting aircraft types naturally creates some efficiency compromises on certain flights, but overall it dramatically impacts the costs associated with the following:

- Maintenance procedures are more easily trained

- Parts inventory is significantly lower

- Pilot and attendant training is less complex

- Ticketing software is simpler and easier to understand

Southwest can more easily handle the day-to-day issues of providing air travel services, such as when an aircraft has a mechanical need or a pilot calls in sick. Can they replace the plane with another one and still accommodate all the passengers? Can they substitute any pilot? The answers to both are much more likely to be "yes".

AMENITIES

Southwest Airlines is not famous for its amenities. It's famous for its *lack* of amenities. Sounds counterintuitive, doesn't it?

Consider this scenario. A Southwest Airlines corporate sales executive comes back to the office and he is very excited about an enormous opportunity. "XYZ Corp is promising to assign their $50 million air travel budget to Southwest exclusively, IF Southwest will agree to provide their employees with priority boarding and assigned seating. Can we do it?!"

This is a pivotal service design and remarkable leadership moment. No doubt that you have faced a similar decision moment in your business. You're anxious for revenue, you've got a big opportunity, but it's going to require some changes and exceptions to how you normally run your business. Sometimes these moments are springboard growth opportunities that genuinely fit, but just as often they are not. What they are, in fact, are tests of your leadership resolve and the boundaries of your remarkable territory.

Now since most companies and leaders have not defined their remarkable territory, these challenges are not recognized as the watershed moments they are. These are the types of daily decisions that can erode your culture, disengage your team, and pit you in a race to the bottom.

GRAB IT

Deciding to make an exception to normal business operations in exchange for increased short-term revenue will feel good. The manager devil on your shoulder will be screaming for you to "grab it!" Unless there is a genuine fit that allows you to expand the boundaries of your Remarkable territory, there are substantial long-term effects to this kind of decision-making - and Remarkability isn't likely to be one of them.

People are drawn to Southwest Airlines because they know what it is, they know what to expect, and then they get it. Southwest benefits from their focus in simplicity and cost advantages.

Can you imagine the ripple effect of trying to implement that $50 million dollar contract opportunity? Can you imagine the reaction of all the other loyal passengers that checked in online for a "Boarding Group A" pass, only to learn they were now second in line to some 'VIP's? I'm not predicting friendly skies.

EMPLOYEE MANAGEMENT

You have no doubt had the experience of standing at the counter of an airline while a sour faced employee slams keys on a hidden keyboard in a fare code language that nobody – including the airline employee - understands.

Have you ever gotten two different answers to the same question from two different agents? Have they ever told you that you have a YZ fare, which has now been changed to an FU fare? Or something like that?

How do you write usable software for thousands of flights, for dozens of aircraft types, three to four different seating areas, special meals and thousands of other small variables?

Imagine trying to make significant changes in that environment. Now imagine trying to actually implement those changes that require retraining thousands of reservation and counter staff, integrating with an already overly complex IT infrastructure, communicating with customers… I get a headache just thinking about it. Is it any wonder that most airlines cannot deliver consistently good service? Of course not… they aren't <u>designed</u> to!

With complex systems like this, what types of people must they employ? What are their job descriptions? How will you find them? How much will you pay them?

Companies without a Remarkable Territory end up with higher costs because they try to fix design problems with attitude and aptitude through their hiring practices. They think that if they hire employees with enough ability and attitude they will be able to overcome any situation.

Employees highest in aptitude AND attitude are not in abundant supply and they absolutely command higher compensation. Even if you can find and afford them, they still may not be able to overcome poor service design; remember the bank executive example. Even *she* was yelling back by the end of the day.

I can't count the number of meetings and conversations I have had about how to find the perfect candidate to fill a position that would magically cure some problem.

Reflecting back, if we were honest with ourselves, we would have realized that we were really just creating an expensive work-around for a flaw in our service design. It is amazing the number of problems you don't have to *manage* if you get service design right.

HI	More Expensive	**Most Expensive**
ATTITUDE	Least Expensive	More Expensive
	LO **APTITUDE** **HI**	

In selecting your territory and designing your organization around it, design it for the employees you either have, or ones that are readily available, not the ones you wish you had, or could find.

Design your service for the employees you have and can readily find more of and train, not the fantasy ones.

CUSTOMER MANAGEMENT

Most people overlook that their customers have a role in the purchase of your product or service... they actually have a job to do. One of the interesting insights of service design is that, unlike pure manufacturing, the customer actually participates in the delivery of the service. If we, as customers, don't understand expectations and our responsibilities in the transaction, the service delivery is impaired, and not just for us, but for the people in line behind us and for the employees serving us.

TSA

Imagine you are in the security line at the airport and you come to that fork where you must decide which conveyor to choose. You know where I'm going. Do you pick the one with the suit-wearing professional travelers who have slip off shoes and roll-a-boards? Or do you line up behind that confused elderly couple that signed up for a cruise? Of course you pick the line where the customers know the routine.

TSA has posters and video tutorials and agents shouting reminders to prepare travelers for their upcoming security job, so that the service of 'ensuring our security' goes smoothly.

SELF SERVICE

Let's look at another example from air travel – except this one is actually quite positive. A number of years back, many of the airlines implemented self serve kiosks. Today, most people highly prefer the kiosk to the counter. Why?

Autonomy.

Standing behind the counter takes longer and I can't really see my options. At the kiosk, I can see the seat map and decide if I'd rather go with an aisle in the far back of the plane or risk a window upfront where the middle seat hasn't been reserved yet.

The trick is to answer the question; How do I get customers to behave the way I want them to and have them to like me MORE for it?

The airline saves money by getting me to do a ticket agent's job, AND I prefer it! Their lower cost alternative is preferable to me. That's a win-win, and an excellent funding technique.

Contrast that with the supermarket's attempts to get us to do self-checkout. Most people avoid this like the plague because it is harder than going through the normal line. It may save the grocer money, but the controls they need to have in place to prevent shoplifting make the solution unpalatable for most shoppers.

The big question to ask yourself when thinking about customer management is; "How do I get customers to behave the way I want, AND have them like me more for it?" The airline kiosk is a great example of this.

SERVICE DESIGN SUMMARY

Remarkable Focus	Employee Management
Customer Management	Funding Mechanism

Service Design from a functional standpoint is an alignment of the organization so that the parts work synergistically. Too frequently this is not the case. When focus is too 'flexible' it brings in customers and requirements that expand the list of things the organization is now expected to do well.

This focus creep stresses systems, resources and employee capabilities to the point where service loses its consistency and the 'rules of the game' become difficult to understand.

As a result, a whole suite of symptoms arise; upset customers, stressed employees, higher defect rates, and higher costs.

From the root cause of service design dysfunction, we grow even more negative side effects; employee turnover, low morale, price pressure, higher customer acquisition costs, and lower margins to name a few.

Consider for a moment, American Airlines which seems to be in a perpetual state of near or actual bankruptcy. Why? American Airlines is a complex beast that lost its focus and found itself in a place where it is trying to do too much.

American Airlines is simultaneously trying to provide the highest service for their most loyal business travelers and compete on cost for the rest of their business. They seem to be caught in the middle on so many very expensive business decisions, and the natural result is an inconsistent customer experience with frustrated employees in a high cost structure (to attempt so much) in a low price environment.

I am using the American Airlines example because it is so well known, but I don't want you to think that their woes are simply because they are in the airline industry or because they are so big. I can show you Mom and Pop restaurants with the same problem. Service design is not well understood, so getting it right is in an opportunity to excel in your industry or market no matter how big or small your business or your market are.

CULTURE

Proper service design alone can do wonders for any organization, but the path to remarkability requires that we get the culture part of leadership right. Culture is a word that gets thrown around a lot, but most of the instruction on it has felt too vague for me. The next three parts of the Remarkable Method are going to specifically identify three human needs that you can satisfy to create a culture that will not only make your organization and you more remarkable, they will also make your life *easier* and give you a huge competitive advantage.

> *"Culture dictates how your employees will behave in your absence"*
> - Harvard Professor Frances Frei

We have looked at what drives us as humans and how important it is for leaders to tap into intrinsic drive. The antithesis of leadership is the 'management mindset'. Leadership and the management mindset are both ways to create a culture.

The management mindset relies on carrots in an attempt to keep the troops 'happy' by using benefits, posters, free snacks and other extrinsic rewards. Every once in a while, a management mindset culture might even sprinkle in a "team building" event. I call this 'forced family fun'. This is where you have a cookout or an "offsite" with the hope of forging some bonds that will improve harmony, loyalty and productivity. Let's just face it and admit that most applications of these tactics are about as effective as giving your mate flowers because you believe that's all it takes to make someone love you.

Bandaids... Hacking.

MANAGEMENT POLICE

The management mindset creates rules and enforces them with sticks. Those rules suck the intrinsic value out of the work environment and create the soulless, bitter place that 75% of our workforce says they are disengaged from.

Guidelines, processes, and procedures all have a place. But they need to be consistent with leadership actions. Sadly, too many management teams do not practice what they preach, and delude themselves into thinking that the conflicts between their words and their behaviors are not detected by their teams.

I can't overstate the importance of culture. Culture is the byproduct of our leadership. The rub is that a 'management mindset' approaches culture from a command and control perspective. It says, "If culture is how my employees behave when I am not there, then I must create rules, so they will know how to behave when I am not there."

What the 'management mindset" leaves out of the statement is that their own behavior is not a sufficient guide.

"Do as I say, not as I do", is not effective leadership

CULTURAL ORIGIN

The real cultural juice is the sum of the signals sent by leadership, which tells the team how to behave, how to think, and most importantly, where they stand. They can be subtle, they are often accidental, but make no mistake, this is where culture comes from.

Remember, we are tribal beings; we want to fit in, so people look to and emulate their tribal leader. Everything that we say and do is a behavioral clue.

If you are a parent, or if you have a pet dog, you have no doubt noticed that you are constantly being watched for clues about expectations. You can literally lead without speaking, and you're leading even when you don't realize it.

My wife Shelly and I, along with all parents I think, are often surprised about some of the things our daughters say. Where on earth did she pick that up? Why does she think that's so important?

The answer of course is often that they saw or heard Shelly or I or a teacher do or say something that seemed important, and she adopted it. Why you ask? **TO FIT IN, to belong.** Fitting in and belonging are enormous human needs.

SIGNALS

> *Arguments by managers that value statements are irrelevant or inappropriate miss the point: All organizations have values; the only question is how explicit they are about them.*
> – O'Reilley and Pfeffer, Hidden Value

Everything that we do or say sends a signal. The sum of our signals dictates how our team will behave when we are not present. The key to being a remarkable leader lies in how your team makes decisions and acts *when neither you, the carrots, nor the sticks are there.*

The good news about culture is that, despite lots of teaching to the contrary, you can change it quickly.

WORK WITH NATURE

If you want to make your leadership remarkable, then the 'rules' of 'fitting in' for your team must be aligned with how you want your team to behave when you are not there. It sounds simple, and in many ways it is, but it is amazing how often our own actions are inconsistent with our true intentions.

The reason we can be inconsistent as managers is because we often don't consciously lead from a place of deep personal purpose. As a result, we abandon our employees and even ourselves on a daily basis. This affects the signals we send to our team, and in turn, affects our culture.

The way to be the most consistent and effective is to lead from a place of higher purpose. When you do this you will be consistently sending the 'right' message. And you won't have to fall back on 'management' tactics to 'control' behavior.

No carrots, no sticks, just you and a team that is enthusiastic about working with and for a leader whose cause resonates with them, and in a work environment that provides them with lots of autonomy. This way your team gets to feel great about why they come to work AND the work itself.

GREAT SERVICE COSTS LESS

I should note here that companies with the greatest service results operate at labor rates that are *below average*! Yes, you heard me right. In his book, What Americans Really Want…Really, Dr. Frank Luntz found in one poll that 84% of Americans said; *"I'd rather make a lot less money at a job I love than more at a job I hate"*.

I'm not suggesting this as a labor expense reduction strategy, but it's interesting to note that total compensation costs skyrocket in organizations where culture and service design are worst. Why? Because in the absence of true employee happiness and proper service design, the Golden Carrot is the 'go to' tool in a 'management mindset' culture. Need evidence of this? Take a look at the union labor disputes taking place around the country.

The organizations that are engaged in painful negotiations with their unions are mostly bureaucratic states and corporations that are not exactly Remarkability Hall of Fame hopefuls. Unions are as anti-autonomy as the management they were meant to protect their members from.

REMARKABLE ELEMENT #2 - INSPIRATION
SOMETHING TO BELIEVE IN

People don't believe what you tell them.
They rarely believe what you show them.
They often believe what their friends tell them
They always believe what they tell themselves.
What leaders do: they give people stories they
can tell themselves. Stories about the future and
about change.

– SETH GODIN

One of the principle tenants of management is to avoid getting emotional and to not get too involved. This makes perfect sense if you consider that our basic business framework was born on the factory floor. The science of management was, after all, developed to maximize throughput of inanimate objects using rudimentary skills and limited intelligence.

It's not a coalmine, but a soul mine…
the canary would wilt in the first meeting.

– STAN SLAP AUTHOR OF BURY MY HEART
IN CONFERENCE ROOM B"

I can't count how many management meetings I have been in where someone said or implied that money was the key motivator of people. "People are coin operated" is one of my favorites. Very, very few people are *really* coin operated once basic needs are met.

All people are values operated. By this I mean that everyone operates based upon the need to satisfy his or her highest values. That intrinsic motivation we talked about earlier is fueled by this very deep inner need.

If you consider the hours spent working – office time, commuting time, and thinking time, we spend more than half of our waking hours devoted to work. You don't get that time back, ever. To not express and engage in a bigger purpose during all that time is a crime and a waste of human potential.

IRONY

Ironically it takes far more energy to detach than to commit. The effort it takes to erect and sustain a wall between our inner purpose and our outer management 'game face' saps energy that cannot be used for better purposes.

Most corporate cultures are designed to stop their would-be leaders from giving. As you examine companies, you find that an overwhelming majority of people choose family and integrity as their highest priorities, AND will report that those same highest priorities are consistently compromised in order to do their jobs successfully.

FILE UNDER: BIG TROUBLE

I want enough personal energy left at the end of the day so the rest of my life isn't just a work-release program.

I want respect

I want control

I want impact

I want a reason to believe – Stan Slap, author of Bury my Heart in Conference Room B

THE ULTIMATE POWER

Committing to a cause that has wide implications and deep personal meaning is an even greater experience than obtaining the combination of intelligence, financial and physical commitment most organizations seek.

This level of commitment solves unsolvable problems and adapts to change in ways that 'management' simply cannot. It is the antidote for the disengagement, and its power is most apparent when an organization needs it most.

Ask yourself:

> *"How much time am I spending managing symptoms of disengagement versus creating a remarkable environment?"*

Often times when executives think about culture they look for tactics to emulate. A notorious example is employee of the month. But if we adopt one of these ideas and it doesn't truly resonate with who we are and what we stand for, then we probably won't stick with it. Few things break trust more effectively than flavor of the month.

When you tap into your personal bigger reason to go to work and lead you will know which ideas fit you and excite you enough to become consistent and reliable parts of your culture. And they will grow into the bigger reason for great employees to join your team, to stay, and to bring and share their best.

Remarkable leaders and organizations achieve high levels of commitment and engagement. And this level of engagement becomes a powerful attractive force for customers and a tremendous competitive advantage.

REMARKABLE ELEMENT #3 – TRIBAL PLATFORM

Great service design requires a culture capable of pulling it off, and that requires cult like dedication.

> **Culture:** the quality in an organization that arises from a concern for what is regarded as excellent… business pursuits, etc.
>
> **Cult:** a group having an exclusive ideology

The good news is that despite jokes to the contrary, people actually like to belong to cults. Facebook, Twitter, Linkedin and many other social media phenomena are thriving exactly because of this - they supply a means for people to belong and connect with causes and ideologies that are important to them.

As we transition from the industrial economy to the Remarkable Economy, people are focusing less and less on quantity and more and more on the quality of the experience.

The most remarkable businesses have turned their customer lists into a membership list. This is what engagement looks like!

Here is what people are looking for in a tribe;

1. To **belong** to a group

2. To be **inspired** by the group's cause

3. To become **valued** as a member of the group

And the mechanism looks like this;

1. Members connected to a leader's cause

2. Leader communicating with members

3. Members communicating with members

4. Members communicating back to their leader

The first key then is to create a mechanism that brings the people that believe in your mission, together. There are as many ways to do this as there are leaders and tribes.

Harley Davidson has Sturgis and Loudon. Jimmy Buffet's Parrot heads convene at tailgate parties, have networking groups, and all kinds of online forums. Schools have homecomings, alumni associations and reunions.

You know about these of course, but what you perhaps haven't unlocked yet is a way to create *your* thing; the mechanism(s) for developing, communicating, and building support for your inspiring cause.

The wonderful challenge and opportunity of this new economy is that we suddenly have tremendous quantities of two things;

1. People who want to engage in more meaningful work.

2. The technology to communicate and assemble.

Businesses that do not adapt to these two overwhelming trends will increasingly be passed over in favor of those that do. Period.

CHALLENGE

So you're going to develop your bigger reason to be followed, and then you're going to work on some creative ways to bring your tribe together, right?

Great! But there is a vital ingredient that I want you to know about.

We all want to master something, to discover our true greatest talents and to attain a level of mastery through practice. When we do this we recognize greatness in ourselves, and others recognize it in us.

Having our own greatness and uniqueness acknowledged provides us with immeasurable power and validation. You feel it in your core and are profoundly impacted in a deep and meaningful way.

Belonging to a group that wouldn't notice if we came or went, well, that wouldn't be much of a group would it? Part of engaging your tribe is making sure that they have an important job in furthering your cause.

When team members are not able to use their strengths at work, chances are that they will;

- Dread going to work

- Have more negative interactions with coworkers

- Treat customers poorly

- Tell friends what a miserable company they work at

- Achieve less on a daily basis

- Have fewer positive and creative moments

There are two lenses that I want you to view this from;

The first is in terms of you. What are your natural talents? Where should you be investing your time and energy.

The second is in terms of your followers. What talents do they have that can be used to further the mission of the tribe?

Please understand that I am not suggesting that you have to custom tailor every job and employee in your company to perfectly suit everyone's strength's. What I am saying is this; find a bigger why for your team to rally around.

The more ways your members have to engage the better. Water will seek its own level, tribal needs and talents will find each other if you create an environment that fosters participation.

FAT BASTARD

Given the negative results of not using your strengths and not working with autonomy, is it any wonder that 75% of the American work force reports being disengaged at work? Is it any wonder that customer service is poor? Is it any wonder that the job of a business leader can so easily deteriorate into a management struggle to get the "unwilling to do the impossible"?

Look again at the previous list. How does a person whose work doesn't allow them to tap into their personal talents feel about themselves, about life, about business, and perhaps about you as their leader?

And where are those feelings channeled? Is it at least possible that of our health and economic problems stem from disengagement coping mechanisms?

> *"I can't stop eating. I eat because I'm unhappy, and I'm unhappy because I eat. It's a vicious cycle. Now, if you'll excuse me, there's someone I'd like to get in touch with and forgive... myself."*
> Fat bastard from the Spy Who Shagged Me

MORE GOOD INSTEAD OF LESS BAD

What does the knowledge about leading from true intention tell us about what's possible? What if you and your company created more ways for you, your team, and your customers to feel great about making your product or service a part of their lives?

Let's go back to our traditional notion of success and my premise that it is a hollow goal. Being successful doesn't require working from a place of true intention. Really *all* you have to do to be successful is just manage the dysfunction better than your competitors. But, and it's a big but, there are two major problems with this:

One, it's mentally, physically and spiritually exhausting. You may earn a lot of money along the way, but the total price paid in terms of health, relationships, and satisfaction is often very high indeed.

Two, changes in the economy, technology, and attitudes are making it possible and ever more likely that you will be faced with a competitor who is leading from a position of true intention.

Succeeding against that competitor is going to be incredibly difficult…unless you learn to lead from intention, and to find ways for more and more of your team to do the same.

Working from this perspective is a key difference between just being successful and the joy of becoming Remarkable. Being successful is doing a good enough job to earn a living and being able to claim above average status. The story of the doctor who didn't really want to be a doctor, but did because *doctors make a good living*, is a cliché that has a strong basis in reality.

The bar is rising quickly as customers and employees demand higher levels of authenticity and engagement. This competitive threat is only going to become more and more prevalent. As people redirect their professions in more satisfying and congruent ways, more potent competitors will emerge.

Being remarkable is operating at an entirely different level. A level that is mentally, physically and spiritually energizing. A level that is sustainable, rewarding and damn fun.

SUMMARY

Your bigger why is the inspiring reason to join your tribe, but it's your tribal platform that creates opportunities for your members to help further your cause.

The glue to keeping members engaged comes from providing opportunities to challenge themselves. Everyone wants to feel needed. Providing your members with a meaningful way to contribute gives them feelings of self worth, and it gives you their support and loyalty.

REMARKABLE ELEMENT #4 – ALIGNMENT

THE CORPORATE ORGANISM

A business is a living organism. It's people are it cells and its departments are its organs which combine to create this living breathing wonder that people spend more than half of their waking hours attending to.

Yet somehow, most managers see their employees and the company as separable elements. The cells require a healthy host to thrive, and the host requires healthy cells. It's a symbiotic relationship, or at least it should be.

But in the absence of aligned leadership, employees and customers remain unorganized self-interested 'free radicals' rather than an intrinsically motivated tribe. So the corporate organism bribes, bullies and bluffs in its quest to attain financial, physical and intellectual commitment from employees. If this reminds you of the predominant medical paradigm for treating our physical bodies *after* they get sick, then you are getting the extent to which we have been *fighting* human nature instead of working with it.

The behavior of teams is only unpredictable and dangerous if you don't start from a human perspective to begin with. Your company's performance is hardwired to the hearts of your team.

Remarkable leaders hardwire their service design and their purpose, so that their hearts, the hearts of their team AND the heart of their organization are hardwired together.

Proper service design makes a business run much more smoothly. Done well, service design creates a noticeably more reliable service experience. Being reliable is THE key to deeply satisfying not only customers, but also employees. The heart of great service isn't in the magnitude of unexpected upside surprises, its heart is in consistency.

Creating a company that is capable of enduring with scalable consistency takes disciplined leadership. Here is where we get to the linchpin in the Remarkable Method.

Discipline, to me, carries with it connotations of trying to maintain unnatural habits. I don't know many people who can consistently will themselves to work against their nature for days let alone decades, and I'm not going to ask you to do that.

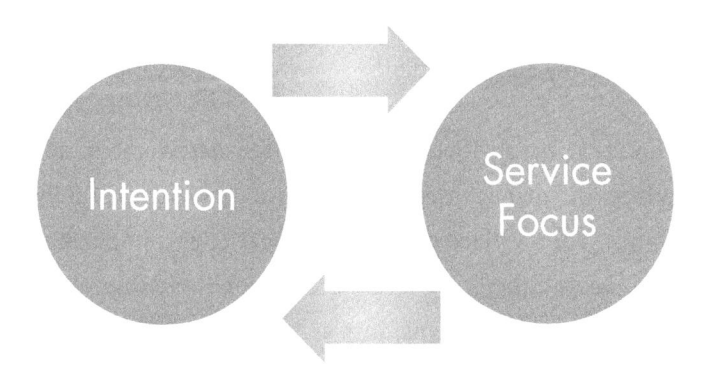

"Our principles are our procedures and our procedures are our principles"

- CJ Mertz

Leadership gets a lot easier when doing what you value is the same thing that makes your business run smoothly and also fills the values of your tribe (team and customers). The best part is that performance comes along for the ride.

A purpose-centered leader creates a purpose-centered organization made up of a purpose-centered team. And this is the kind of organization that is capable of focus, and of remarkable service design.

Your leadership mission (which we will get to in a moment) is identifying and articulating that inspiring cause, and it is your leadership that creates the tribe. Here is the good news. Because you will be leading from a place that is deeply and naturally you…guess what?... consistency will be a snap!

The very reason that leadership often deteriorates into symptom management is because leadership rarely comes from a place of deep personal congruency. It is very, very difficult to lead based upon someone else's values and expectations, just as it is difficult to build a company that is all things to all customers.

The key to creating a remarkable culture is to tap into a cause that is deeply inspirational to you and to lead from that place. Since it will be so deep and so personal, you won't need to be reminded to do it and it won't require some super human discipline to behave in an unnatural way. Your genuine consistency will become a magnet and a beacon to the followers of your tribe.

LEADERSHIP

There are a lot of myths about leadership; it's a burden, you have to be born with the ability, you have to become someone you're not. None of this is true. If leadership was such a bad thing, no one would do it. If you had to be a certain personality type, then there wouldn't be so many different kinds of leaders. If you think about history's most remarkable leaders, most of them did it for *free*.

Leadership is actually a benefit. In fact it's a series of benefits that you can only get by doing what remarkable leaders do; leading from a personal center of belief that is truly yours.

The purpose of leadership is to change the world in the name of your purpose. In turn, you get to live and work in greater alignment with your values.

You - as an already successful business leader - have a great opportunity and a head start. You already have some resources and a vehicle for leadership expression. Your business and your career are a canvas for contribution and fulfillment, and there is a flock of would be followers who are impatient for you to get on with it.

REMARKABLE RECAP
MISSION DIFFERENTIATION

The most sustainable and powerful differentiation you have is not in your product or service solution set at all. It is inside of you. It IS you. Specifically, it is your inspired purpose. Your values point to a personal mission that can add massive meaning to your leadership. The more congruent you are with your own unique purpose, the more confidence and purpose you will inspire in yourself and your team.

People who are focused on their life's mission draw opportunities. Their certainty of who they are and where they are going, acts as a drawing card for others to align and assist. People love to be around those who are purposeful.

- Dr. John F. Demartini

People love to be around remarkable people. And remarkable people benefit from a tailwind of support that successful people do not because they are literally riding *with* the flow. The strategic decision to pursue remarkability makes your business and your life run more smoothly, and it puts less pressure on executing your tactics perfectly because you will be leading a team that is *engaged*, rather than disengaged.

TO BE VALUED

We are motivated to perform when our work expresses who we are, when the business' goals are intrinsically meaningful to us, and we feel that we are valued as people, not simply as economic agents.

- Charles A. O'Reilly III and Jeffrey Pfeffer, Hidden Value

We are tribal by nature. We have a deep seeded need to 'belong' to something greater than ourselves. In evolutionary and biological terms, this need to belong was an adaptation for self-preservation. In our earlier days as humans the tribe was a source of protection and food.

We hunted and gathered together, we ate together, we raised our young together and we fought against predators and enemies together. This support structure was required to survive. Not fitting in was a good way to get kicked out, and getting kicked out was good way to die.

"Fit in = Live" is hardwired into us somehow.

TIPPING POINT

The defining moment of this time is the tipping point between fitting in and being ourselves, the clash between disengagement and engagement, the clash between masking symptoms and addressing root causes. We are in the process of integrating who we are with what we do on a mass scale.

Historically, being different was heresy, and being an agent of change was a ticket to loneliness. But today, the internet makes the world our village. This means that I can find people who don't 'fit in' in the same way that I don't 'fit in' pretty easily. We can be our own tribe of people who didn't 'fit in', but now do! Technology not only protects us from the ravages of nature, it also enables us to realize tribal comfort from our desktop.

LINKING IT TOGETHER

You are a leader.

You have a purposeful mission or cause.

People are looking to align themselves with a leader who has certainty in who they are and a cause they can resonate with.

Your cause can be both your inspiration AND theirs.

Consider that Martin Luther King had a dream that he was willing to die for. His commitment and the fact that his cause resonated with so many became a force that attracted followers and support. Did all of his supporters have the same values he did? No, but supporting his dream enabled them to live their values while also feeling that they were an important part of something bigger than themselves.

Don't worry about the scope of *your* mission - your dream may not be to solve racial inequality, but I'm betting that you have a cause within you that can and will resonate with a surprisingly large number of people and that can form the nucleus of *your* tribe.

Your leadership can turn your employee and customer list into a tribal following.

Your leadership can form a culture capable of staying focused on being remarkable in your market.

That remarkable service consistency combined with your mission-centered leadership will cause you to deliver ever-greater value to ever-greater numbers of people.

Remember that a remarkable leader is a person who has cleverly **infused** their **mission** into their **career** and created a **loyal following** by delivering **massive value** through **focused service design.**

Become a leader with more than a product or service. Become a leader of a cause.

Give me a reason to want to follow you besides earning a paycheck for myself and profits for the company.

Provide me with an opportunity to play a role that makes me feel valued.

Align the focus of your company with your personal intention.

Pursue remarkability, be the antidote to disengagement, make a difference in the quality of life of your tribe, and contribute to society's wealth, freedom, and fulfillment.

TWO
REMARKABLE STORIES

The Industrial Revolution gave us a lot of great things. But its hangover is the brute force management mindset which defaults to command and control, carrots, and sticks whenever it encounters resistance.

The problem is that business today IS change, and tasks that cannot be automated by computers and machines are left to people. The management mindset is conflicted;

It wants to command and control; AND it wants its employees to think on their feet, be happy, and be productive.

Management asks employees to bring the best of themselves to work each day, to "behave well in the absence of management", and then it denies them the sources of motivation to do so. There are two common sources of this conflict;

The first is structural. The service design of many organizations is such that even the most competent and motivated employees get burned out. The impatient nature of the management mindset is too willing to compromise service design for revenue.

The second is cultural. The management mindset leaves little room for intrinsic motivation. It places money before intention. The problem is that intention does not follow money, money follows intention. Companies that believe that they can pursue money first and expect harmony later end up with the most disharmony.

The solution is remarkable leadership; a combination of focused service design and culture that together creates an environment for successful and repeatable service, along with personal fulfillment.

A remarkable leader builds an organization that engages its tribe and develops two enormous competitive advantages;

1. Loyalty

2. Economy

Plain and simple, a remarkable service design eliminates a whole host of issues that non-remarkable organizations spend inordinate amounts of time and resources attempting to 'control and manage'.

REMARKABLE REWARDS

An amazing thing happens when a business is focused, inspired, tribal and aligned. Employees show up in uncommon ways. Service improves, products improve, and customers notice. Not only that, the meaning that inspires this performance becomes palpable and contagious.

Human lives are impacted by this and stories emerge. Customers, employees, and community members begin to 'remark' about this unusual place. And then the support snowball begins; referrals, loyalty, and new opportunities.

With a greater purpose to focus on and greater service alignment, employee management issues diminish and energy that would have been spent on defensive issues is now available for offensive initiatives.

This next section contains some real examples of Remarkable principles in practice. The organizations are diverse; a chiropractic clinic, an industrial vibrator company, a regional transit authority and a gym.

Relative to the Fortune 1000, each company is on the small side with total team size between 10 and 1,000. This is on purpose. You've already seen stories about Nordstroms, Zappos, and the Four Seasons. Their service stories are well known.

I chose examples this size because I want to demonstrate that the remarkable method can be applied in small organizations, even solo entrepreneurs can apply the principles. In fact smaller organizations actually have advantages that larger organizations do not.

The companies I am about to feature are in different industries and the leaders have very different leadership styles. Remarkable leadership is not a personality type and it's not industry dependent. You can become a remarkable leader and make your organization remarkable regardless of your industry and regardless of your personality.

"DOC" FRANSON
PURPOSE

When you first meet Dr. Stephen Franson of Franson Family Chiropractic you know immediately that you're dealing with a man on a mission.

Dr. Stephen is totally committed to educating and adjusting as many families as possible through natural chiropractic care, and dedicated to eating, moving and thinking well so he can authentically lead others to do the same. Anyone who has the privilege of spending time with Dr. Stephen is immediately touched.

Every cell in this man's body operates with the mission to authentically educate and inspire others toward positive, on-purpose, healthy lifestyle change.

If we were talking about being successful, we'd discuss that Dr. Stephen's clinic treats ten times more patients than the average clinic. Incredibly, he sees 800-1000 patients per week. We would talk about revenue and profit, we could talk about his surfboard collection, we would talk about his home, or even his cool "Hell Barn" where he hosts friends and neighbors for challenging workout sessions.

Like most successful people, Dr. Stephen has goals, there is no doubt about it. There is also no doubt about the fact that he is achieving many of them, and well on his way toward new bigger goals.

> **FFC Mission:** Our purpose is to educate and adjust as many families as possible toward optimal health through natural chiropractic care

But Dr. Stephen is beyond successful, he's truly remarkable. He is remarkable because he has organized his practice and his entire life around his purpose - helping people reach their potential. Stephen operates by this motto; "I'd rather lose a patient than lose my integrity." And he means it.

REMARKABLE TERRITORY

> *"Our procedures are our principles are our principles are our procedures."*
> **CJ MERTZ**

During our discussion of Remarkable territory design, we learned about the importance of picking a territory to master. FFC starts with a question; "What factors contribute to patient success?" They build their practice around making sure that patients succeed by providing two key things; chiropractic adjustments and education.

They don't provide ancillary products and services. They don't provide anything except chiropractic adjustments and education. No massage, no physical therapy, no line of supplements, just focused adjustments and education.

Dr. Stephen says, "If you think about it, chiropractic care is unique to start with, the adjustment IS our unique contribution to health." Dr. Stephen wants his patients to remain focused on root causes so he doesn't dilute the treatment experience in any way.

PATIENT MANAGEMENT

FFC goes many steps further however. They know from experience that if a patient does not adopt certain lifestyle habits then all the adjusting in the world will fail to bring them to optimal health. So patients are *required* to attend education sessions.

FFC also knows that if the patient doesn't make adjustments a regular part of their personal maintenance, life will take its course and wellness will slip, so patients book a year's worth of appointments, in advance. Oh, and FFC doesn't accept insurance!

A cynic might say at this point, "Oh, how convenient, what's best for the patient also happens to be best for the practice."

Exactly.

And if it wasn't, do you think patients would actually do it? FFC patients actively recruit family members and friends because of one reason. Results.

Dr. Stephen has put his mission on the line. He and his team must deliver every day for every patient. He knows that he has to do more than just convince people to come back; he has to deliver life-changing results.

By focusing on results for the patient first, Dr. Stephen's practice reaps great rewards. New patients bring friends and family along to share in the experience and results. Results for his patients means results for the clinic, and as you'll see, results at the clinic fund more results for the patient. It's a truly a symbiotic relationship. Just the way it should be.

The staff at FFC go to work to fulfill a mission that they believe in. In return, they get to live their personal values at work.

TRIBE

When individuals share a common purpose, a bond begins to develop that transforms them from a group to a tribe. Along the way, an unspoken accountability and support structure forms.

Education at FFC isn't just a lecture or a DVD, it's a community experience. Dr. Stephen insists that patients attend new patient orientations and ongoing workshops together because he knows from experience that the patient will make more progress with education and each other than without.

As patients sit together in the waiting area they are "edutained" by one of Stephen's many professionally-produced seminars. No *People* magazines here. This place is built for health.

Patient of the Month and Family of the Month profiles adorn the walls. Family - both the patient's immediate family and their greater FFC family -are an obvious theme that you can't overlook. The patients who visit Dr. Stephen are not strangers.

The regular appointment structure supports regular interaction between patients. After a year in the 8 AM Monday time slot, you've gotten to know quite a bit about the people you share that time with.

Personal relationships help to create and foster the FFC community. For example, when FFC wanted to promote great nutrition, the patient community developed a cookbook of healthy recipes. Tribal members sharing with each other is a tremendous way to increase the bond with your cause.

CULTURE

A surfboard is displayed prominently on a wall in Dr. Stephen's office. It is an artifact of Dr. Stephen's love of the ocean and surfing. Each year, Dr. Stephen and his family host a family retreat in a beautiful surf spot like Costa Rica. It's a week of family fun, adventure and health that tightens the tribe and increases results. It gives Dr. Stephen and his family the opportunity to connect with their patients while doing what they love.

> *"I know so many doctors who preach the message of health, and then live horribly contradictory lifestyles. The Doctors and Team Members of this practice do just the opposite. They model it. Their families model it. We live, eat and breathe the stuff we teach!!"*
> FFC Staffer, Alexis

Stephen does practice what he preaches and he insists that his team does as well. Their daily schedule is designed to ensure time for healthy snack breaks, personal errands and even a quick nap. How many doctors' offices have you visited where the staff was grouchy and unhealthy? Is their business focus health or revenue. Are their actions congruent with ensuring your wellness? Are their patients happy? Is their staff engaged? Typically, NO!

How can you be in the health business and not be healthy? The truth is that we can't be Remarkable in any endeavor – business, sport, or otherwise - where we don't wholeheartedly live our intention. Businesses like FFC stand out as remarkable because so many other businesses compromise personal values and ethics to make a buck.

Dr. Stephen and his team at FFC epitomize the Remarkable Method. They are loving, efficient, professional and competent. They are real with themselves, with each other, and with their patients. That energy affects everyone who visits their practice. I know of no 'management strategy' that approaches this level of effectiveness.

"CAPTAIN" KARL OF LEAN NATION

PURPOSE

It's 8 AM and I'm standing in the lobby of VIBCO Vibrators, a commercial vibration equipment manufacturer, participating in the 'morning stretch meeting'. Karl Wadensten, President of VIBCO, is facilitating a 'stand up and stretch while you update each other' staff meeting.

"Ok, what's on your plate for today?" Says Karl through his ever-present unlit cigar. The updates and discussions continue around the circle, "Ok, now stretch your shoulders… now arms across the chest"…

On paper, VIBCO Vibrators is a run-of-the-mill manufacturer of industrial vibrators with a machine shop, an assembly area, engineering, and front-office operations. You might think there's nothing special about a business like that. You'd be wrong. Very, very wrong. VIBCO Vibrators is actually a canvas for Karl's highest values; Being of service to others, personal growth in Karl's 'Dream Big, Go Big' style, and a heavy dose of showmanship.

> *"You might think there's nothing special about a business like that. You'd be wrong.*
> *Very, very wrong."*

Maybe you wouldn't be surprised that the President of an industrial manufacturing company would be a guy with a cigar in his mouth – it's a tough business, after all. But you would never guess that behind the persona, Karl is all heart and is not afraid to put himself out there. Karl dresses in bright colors, typically jeans or brightly patterned pants and his trademark Lily Pulitzer shirts, a style that makes a statement whenever he enters a room.

A number of years ago, Karl faced the same dilemma that practically every U.S. based manufacturing business has experienced. "How do we keep our jobs here? How can we compete and stay in business?"

Most people accepted the conventional wisdom; move manufacturing overseas. That's the 'management mindset' answer. Karl went with the 'remarkable' answer; "Let's carve a niche and become so good at what we do that our labor cost is no longer an issue. Let's do something novel, something truly remarkable, let's focus on the customer AND the employee!"

REMARKABLE TERRITORY

The 'niche' that Karl and his team selected was "Same Day, Next Day". The traditional approach to manufacturing

– the management mindset - says something like this; "Once you get a machine set up for a certain part, run it for a long time and make enough parts to justify how long it takes to set up the machine. Build inventory even if you didn't need it, because those machines are expensive. They need to be up and running." This mentality was born from one simple constraint, the time it took to set up the machine.

At that critical time for VIBCO, not only were the company's labor costs too high, but they had a constant surplus of some inventory parts and a near-constant deficit of other parts. When a customer needed a product fast, VIBCO Vibrators could only deliver if they got lucky and the customer wanted what they had on the shelf. For the rest, well, "we'll be making a batch of those sometime next week." This was not the right answer for an on-demand world.

The only way to provide a better answer was to reduce machine set-up times from over 2 hours to under 10 minutes. The only way to do that was nothing less than a total organizational commitment to *lean manufacturing*.

If you have any experience with implementing quality improvement methods and/or programs, you know that the talking and planning is easy. The doing? Not so much.

Fast forward through a few years of relentless and remarkable leadership to find VIBCO Vibrators actually living process improvement. They made gigantic improvements in every area of their facility. It was not easy. 95% of companies fail in their lean management implementations because they mistakenly believe that lean is a management initiative to control human behavior.

Most organizations that try to implement lean don't engage the best parts of their employees. They don't engage because the culture doesn't support engagement – it takes away autonomy and mastery, and there isn't a widely understood 'bigger purpose' to the initiative. It's perceived to be only about profit and cost savings.

CULTURE

With lean and many other commitments in life, hesitation kills. It has to be an all out sprint to the other side. Spend too much time in no man's land and your chances of success start dropping… quickly.

Karl and his team needed nothing short of a full commitment. This had to become an organizational passion. Enter Karl's personal values; Being of service to others, personal growth (Dream Big, Go Big style), and a heavy dose of showmanship.

Through Karl's value lens, he didn't see Lean as a management tactic to improve operational performance; he saw it as an opportunity to bring the whole Karl to work AND to improve operational performance. Implementing lean is tough and not necessarily exciting in and of itself, but implementing lean in the name of personal growth IS very exciting for Karl.

What Karl did was a stroke of personal and professional genius. It embodies what being remarkable is all about; he combined his passion with his business. By making *lean* about fulfilling his highest values, his MISSION, he tapped into the unlimited reservoir of energy that he would need to succeed as the leader.

This was Karl's chance to share his passion of personal growth with his entire manufacturing family. He saw this as much more than an organizational necessity. Karl saw lean as nothing less than a golden opportunity for his entire family to grow personally and professionally.

By creating a cause that was bigger than manufacturing industrial vibrators, Karl gave himself and his team a reason to come to work, a reason to do the hard work, and a reason to persevere. By making *lean* about individual growth, Karl tapped into a cause that everyone loved and could sustain - their own personal growth and that of their teammates and families.

Implementing Lean Manufacturing requires that team members learn and develop so many skills that are simply not required in an assembly line manufacturing environment. Lean challenges our skills as observers, communicators, problem solvers, conflict resolvers, public speakers, writers, presenters, teachers, and project managers… just to name a few.

One of the reasons that I feel so passionately about Remarkability is my belief that we can change our society by changing how and why we go to work. 75% of our workforce feels disengaged at work. A similar percentage feel that work is just a continuation of the same disregard for their talents as in their school experience.

I believe that remarkable project leaders will transform our society by transforming the experiences of their teams at work. Give your team a bigger reason to go to work, make their work place one that fills them up rather than depletes them, and watch the world and your bottom line change for the better.

There are many moments at VIBCO Vibrators that have inspired me and literally brought me to tears. One of those moments was when a VIBCO manager told me this story about his work prior to the company's (and more importantly his) lean transformation.

"Work was stressful. It was like we were constantly failing to deliver. We could never have the right parts in the right quantities, and I was always in the middle; Sales and customer service yelling at me on one side and work teams that dreaded my demands for us to work faster on the other side. It was a total lose-lose situation.

I took the stress out on my team and I took it home to my family. One day while I was at work, my family went on a day trip. When I got home, my son gave me this hat with a crab on it. He said this is your crabby Daddy hat. It hurt to hear my son say that.

I wanted out of that environment so I went to school with the intent to improve my resume and go somewhere new. Meanwhile, we began our lean journey and I had an epiphany. I could have control and we could meet customer demands.

I learned all sorts of interpersonal skills that I feel have made me a better leader, father and husband. I don't go home stressed now, in fact I love my job, and talking about it at home is source of happiness.

Now when I go to work I feel like I am a part of something bigger than myself. I feel like I belong to a great team. I feel like what we do matters to customers, and I feel like I am an important part of making it all happen.

And you want to know something crazy? My son is 18 now, and he wants to come work at VIBCO."

Think about that for a moment. Picture a typical 'factory mindset' work environment. Your picture could just as easily be an office, or a restaurant, or a retail store. Just picture it. Now picture how those workers feel about their work, and imagine how that shapes their views of society, of humans, of trust, policy, politics, fairness, opportunity and meaning.

Now imagine how they view the world. Do they go home and tell stories of hope to their children at the dinner table? What stories do they share with their friends? What issues do they vote for? Or against? How do they escape? Do they use food, alcohol, drugs, TV? Engagement changes everything.

You have incredible power as a leader to affect how people think and feel and live. Your opportunity to be remarkable is not just a great business strategy; it also has unimaginable side benefits. Imagine the power of thousands of leaders like Karl Wadensten and Dr. Stephen and what their collective impact is on society. Now imagine what YOUR impact will be.

FUNDING MECHANISM

One prerequisite to succeeding at lean is to allocate a lot of time and resources to the task. Not an easy thing to do when labor costs are already too high! So how do they pay for it?

VIBCO Vibrators has two unique ways that they fund their greatness. The first is their culture which creates the necessary environment and generates the necessary energy to continue to improve. The second is by using their culture as a marketing tool. At VIBCO Vibrators the line between culture and marketing is blurry.

When I first learned about Karl's Lean journey, it was through a workshop event he was running at VIBCO Vibrators which I wasn't able to attend. I had heard about how great it was, so I asked Karl if I could come down to his plant in Rhode Island and see what he was up to.

Karl, in his usual enthusiastic and gracious style said "Absolutely! And bring your team too; you're not going to want them to miss this. We're doing some really great stuff here; you just have to see it."

So I rented a van and we went on a road trip to VIBCO to take a tour. Lean at VIBCO Vibrators begins at the reception desk and ends at the shipping dock... it is EVERYWHERE. We toured the plant in a couple of groups. "Wait a minute" I thought, "you do this every day?"

Our tour went from workstation to workstation. We spoke directly with the line operators, not Karl or a slick marketing tour guide. Each worker explained their personal lean journey, the incredible results they had achieved, and the effect it had on them personally.

At Lucy's station we heard her talk about how many steps, <u>yes Lucy counts her footsteps</u>, it took for her to make a part, and how she was trying a new experiment that she thought would take 5 seconds off her build time. Yes, 5 seconds. In fact at every station the operators spoke of their latest ideas and the seconds they would save.

Lucy shared her story;

> *"You have no idea how hard my job used to be. When I got home at the end of the day my body and brain just felt used and tired. I barely had the energy to make dinner and then collapse in front of the TV.*
>
> *Now when I get home I have energy to spare! I went from leaving myself at work to having myself at both places and not having to choose. At first my husband didn't know what to make of it. Especially when I organized all of his tools and labeled all the drawers, but I think he appreciates it now. I really like my job because I feel*

this sense of accomplishment that I get from solving problems. I'm a happy camper now."

What Lucy didn't say explicitly (but was obvious) is that she used to have a factory job in a factory. She had to stand at a station and make parts till the day ended. It was monotonous and provided little if any 'nutritional' value. Lucy used to be disengaged at work and now she has become *engaged*.

With the advent of lean at VIBCO Vibrators, she has a dynamic, thinking, intelligence-based job… in a factory. She has the responsibility to think about how and why she does what she does, and to also help others do the same. Today Lucy is no longer an economic agent; she is a valued member of a cause that is bigger than her.

Score another point for Remarkability!

I found inspiration in an environment that almost everyone would write off. I was already a believer in Remarkable as a method for building a business and a better world, but I was totally blown away to see Vibco's application of it.

After visiting with Lucy we headed back into the center of the building to Karl's office - a room with an almost 360 view of the entire company - located next door to the studio of The Lean Nation, Karl's former radio – now web television - program.

Today, I and a few of my teammates are going to be guests on Karl's show. This is the routine. Take people on tours, show them what lean is all about and invite make them to be guests on a radio program that is broadcast around the world via live web stream, and of course, throughout the VIBCO plant.

Karl has turned his efforts into a marketing platform. If you want your customers to believe that your quality is the best you have several options. You can claim it in some marketing copy in a brochure or on your website, or you can train your sales staff to say it. But nothing can come close to the impact of turning your company's quest for excellence into a live reality show.

Karl is leading his company the same way he lives, right on his sleeves and right on the edge. How cool is this!? This guy is changing lives, growing personally, promoting his company, making stars of his team, and becoming a celebrity all in one step. Using his creativity and his values, Karl has carved a place for himself on this earth where he gets to be Karl 24/365. And everyone around him wins. How can you not want this kind of life and legacy?!

"BUS DRIVER" MARK

When Mark Aesch took the wheel of the Rochester Genesee Regional Transportation Authority (RGTA), he faced a massive $27.7 million budget deficit. Previous management had seen the financial crisis coming but did nothing to avoid or slow the onset.

*Now, with a total budget of around $70 million, we were cooked. During my first weeks in the corner office, colleagues were advising me that we would survive only if we took not one but **all** of the following drastic steps: raise fares 40 percent across the board, reduce service by 65 percent, double fares on the disabled population we served, and axe about a quarter of our workforce.*[ii]

Those were tough words to hear. The problems at the RGTA were severe and so were the recommended cuts. The problem was compounded by two deeply entrenched unions with a history of non-cooperation.

The union leadership's general attitude toward life on the job back in those days went roughly as follows:

We come in to work. And you're going to pay us. And however much you pay us, we're going to complain about it. And don't even think about measuring our performance. We want 100 percent of our healthcare paid for, but that doesn't count as a benefit.[iii]

We want to be able to not show up for eighteen days in a year, without being sick or on vacation- just not show up- before you can discipline us. We want to be able to take days off, even if we don't have any vacation days left. Sick days will be like vacation days.

And we'll deliver the product in twice the amount of time at four times the cost of the private sector. And don't tell us anything about tough times. There's always been plenty of money. There will always be plenty of money. Just pay us more. Pay us at the highest level of the industry, for mediocre work.

Mark Aesch and his team rejected the idea that the situation was hopeless. They didn't accept that the only solutions were drastic cuts in services and fare hikes. They did what remarkable people do… they threw away the limited choices provided by the management mindset to find a better way to solve the problem.

Remember – management mindset solutions are driven by brute force rules, controls and financial management formulas that are not necessarily a means to sound <u>actual</u> financial performance. In fact, brute force management was the *reason* that the RGTA was in such dire straights.

As Mark quickly observed, the path to solving the RGTA's woes meant totally rethinking who the organization served and how RGTA served them. And he needed to engage the whole team to make all of this possible.

THE COWS GET FED FIRST

Mark spent the first 21 years of his life on a small family farm feeding cows and shoveling their output. When he was a boy, he and his siblings had to get their chores done in the morning before they had breakfast.

On the farm, the animals were their lifeblood. No animals, no farm. No farm, no food. It was simple. Mark's leadership philosophy and values were forged in an environment that put service before self. When he set out to turn the bus company around, it was this service mindset that made the impossible, possible.

REMARKABLE TERRITORY

It was clear from the outset that the RGTA had its priorities upside down. If the authority was excellent at anything, it was in totally avoiding responsibility. Management and the unions didn't claim to be in control or accountable, so it naturally followed that they couldn't be blamed for anything.

Mark saw that the organization needed focus. It was the only way he saw that could actually begin to improve performance. So after some analysis, he and his team decided that RGTA should focus on a very clear goal - providing clean buses that arrived on time.

> *"We had to figure out how to drive fewer miles, and pick up more people who were happier."*
> MARK AESCH

FUNDING MECHANISM

With a ridership of over 18 million passengers, 410 buses and 820 employees, Mark Aesch realized that RGTA needed to improve the quality of data and data analysis so that the incredibly complex operation could run smoothly.

The complexity and depth of the problem also required management by a team that was eager to collect and analyze data, then have frank discussions about real facts. Oh… and they needed more revenue. Desperately.

So Mark and his team decided to invest in data and total team participation. These investments ultimately lead to dramatically improved decision-making about routes, maintaining cleaner buses, and attaining greater on-time performance. Achieving these things pleased their customers, which ultimately increased ridership.

With more, happier riders, the RGTA earned more revenue. With more streamlined operations, they dramatically reduced overtime and other expenses that had been causing significant financial losses.

Here's where it goes from being a successful story to a remarkable one. RGTA's dramatically improved performance, along with a corresponding improved public image, lead to an even bigger source of new revenue - subsidy partners.

Prior to Aesch's involvement, RGTA was an organization with an extremely limited view of itself. It was a public necessity, much like garbage removal and road maintenance. That view stunted their creativity. As you recall, creativity only likes to show up when autonomy is present. You can imagine that creativity had been in short supply in the financially driven bureaucracy that was the pre-Aesch RGTA.

As the focus on data quality and clean, on-time performance showed results, it emboldened and empowered the management team to set out and discover new ways that their service could earn additional revenue.

The RGTA team pursued a deal with the city school district to carry more students to school. The RGTA was already providing this service, but the organization was *losing* sixty cents on every dollar of their $2.4M relationship.

With some creative problem solving, Aesch and his team developed a new strategy that expanded the relationship to an $11.5 million *breakeven* relationship. This was a huge win for both organizations; it enabled the RGTA to keep fares stable, and the school district received bussing for 11,500 students per day with *improved attendance!*

SIDE BENEFITS

One of the great rewards of the Remarkable Method is the side benefits that accompany improved financial results. The school got to improve attendance while reducing bussing costs AND increasing state funding. All it required was for the leadership and people in the process to throw away the limitations of a management mindset and open their thinking to the limitless opportunities for collaboration and synergy.

Stop and think for a moment about how toxic it must have been to work in the bureaucratic unionized culture of RGTA, as it was when Mark Aesch arrived. The disadvantages to taxpayers and management are obvious. But what about those 810 employees? What were the effects on them? Their families? And how about the 18 million riders, most of whom rely upon the RGTA as their sole means of transportation? Their 'car' now shows up on time, there isn't trash rolling along the floor, and they don't have to worry about sitting in people's used chewing gum.

Remarkability is a renewable energy source. It's a positive feedback loop. The more remarkable the culture the more creativity and initiative is given back and the greater the results and satisfaction.

The beliefs of RGTA employees and the beliefs of their families about life and meaning were largely shaped by their experiences at RGTA. What did that toxic culture teach them about what is possible in business and in life? How about their faith in management? In each other?

It's great that the RGTA has achieved amazing financial and performance results. As taxpayers, we all owe Mark and his team our thanks and appreciation, but being remarkable goes way beyond just the financial results. It's these very results that make Remarkability a renewable energy source.

CAESAR MCFADDEN

Caesar McFadden is a famous character at the RGTA. Caesar was the archetype that defined the relationship between the unions and management when Mark began as CEO.

At his first meeting with the entire RGTA, Aesch had a showdown with McFadden in front of the whole organization. Mark describes Caesar McFadden as an intimidating-looking figure - over six feet five inches, about 350 lbs, wearing gold earrings and a heavy assortment of gold chains, one of which was a placard around his neck that read "LIAR" in big, block letters.

At the meeting, Caesar McFadden loudly questioned Mark's plans and accused him of not caring about Caesar and his co-workers. McFadden said, "You people don't give a damn about us! You don't know what we go through every day. You don't care about our bills, our families!"

Mark resolutely stood his ground through all of the interruptions. Caesar, along with the union boss and the rest of the union members, ultimately ended up storming out of the room. To his credit, Mark didn't give in or give up.

That unwavering commitment to his vision was an essential piece of the puzzle for Aesch, his team, and the RGTA. Two years later, Mark and his team prepared to submit their Comprehensive Plan to the board. Traditionally, only the CEO and the CFO signed and submitted the plan. Mark, in accordance with a 'no ego' team philosophy, decided that whole team should sign the plan. At a company-wide event celebrating their accomplishments, Mark made his announcement:

"If you feel like you helped this year, if you feel like you got out in front of the wagon and pulled to get us through the mud when we were stuck, then I want you to sign the letter."

With balloons still falling, U2's "Beautiful Day" still playing, and our employees congratulating one another and milling about, Caesar McFadden made his way over to me.

"Look, I'm not signing the letter."

"Here we go," I thought. There was no way a guy like McFadden was going to bring me down on a day like this. "That's ok, Caesar," I said. "It's totally up to you."

"But let me tell you why," he said, interrupting. "I'm not gonna sign the letter because I can't."

For a second I wondered if Caesar didn't have the ability to read or write. Sadly, some of our employees don't.

"I'm not going to sign the letter," he continued, "because I didn't believe. I was a disruption. I was embarrassing. I didn't help move us forward. I took shots. I sat back and watched." He opened his eyes wide, looking right at me. "I don't deserve to sign the letter. But next year—next year, that's gonna change. I will believe. I will honor what we do. I will help."[iv]

If a remarkable culture can crack a tough nut like Caesar McFadden, you can turn your toughest critics into your greatest leaders and assets, like Caesar McFadden is now. Can you imagine the lessons and the impact of his honesty and bravery? Detractors like Caesar can be debilitating, but with perseverance they can be brought onto your side, and when they are, their loyalty is incredibly powerful.

Autonomy has great power. Even people with cynical and selfish behavior, at their core, want to be a part of something greater than them. The impact of these transformations is so great, so far reaching, that there is no doubt that it's time for remarkable leadership to take over from the management mindset.

It's time to begin a Remarkable Revolution to restore and preserve the entrepreneurial tradition of increasing freedom and quality of life. It's time for a new business growth paradigm….it's time for a remarkable method of management and leadership.

"COACH" GLASSMAN
SIX AM

It's almost six in the morning and my wife Shelly has just pulled into the garage after her morning workout at Crossfit, the car is still running. I ask her, "How'd you do?", she has a huge smile on her face as she says, "Great! It was tough." We laugh because they're all tough and we think it's funny that we still bother to state the obvious. I give her a kiss and jump in the car to get to the gym in time.

When I get there, my 6:00 am friends are already warming up, massaging their legs and backs over foam rollers. We exchange "good mornings" and banter about the upcoming WOD (Workout of the Day).

There is a nervous tension in the air because we all know that the buzzer will go off very soon, and it will be show time. Our butts and our egos will be on the line. Our friends will be watching, we will be watching, and we want to do our best for ourselves, and believe it or not, for each other.

The room is a random bunch. It's hard to peg a Crossfit crowd. Our group includes doctors, teachers, software developers, engineers, CEO's, bar tenders, waitresses, firemen… really people from all walks of life. We have 20-somethings all the way up to grandparents. But the

6:00 am class is mostly 30- and 40-somethings trying to regain our 20-something bodies, and today is one more shot at that elusive goal.

We are about to begin a 6-week Paleo challenge, named for the Crossfit diet of choice. This morning we will all do a couple maximum repetition tests and a benchmark WOD. I look up at the board, to confirm what I already know. I saw it online last night, and checked it again this morning.

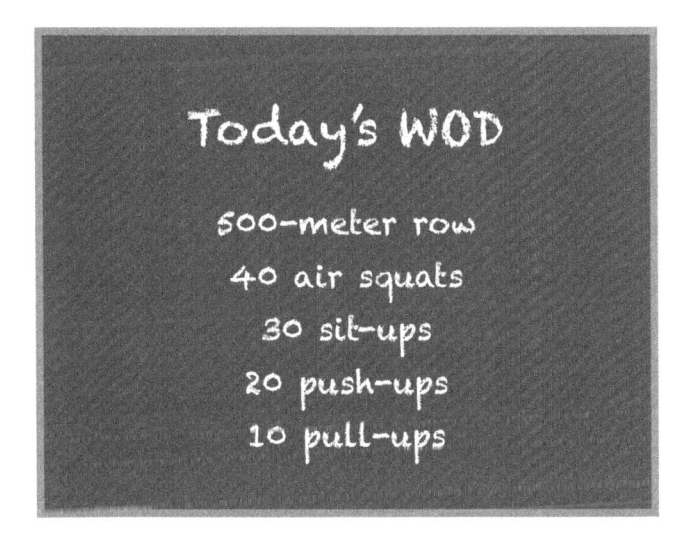

> **Today's WOD**
>
> 500-meter row
> 40 air squats
> 30 sit-ups
> 20 push-ups
> 10 pull-ups

Why? Because that's how addictive Crossfit is. "Uggh" I think to myself, "max pull ups and then we have to do more for speed during the test?!"

Eric, our trainer, coach, and cheerleader takes us through a warm-up to get our bodies ready for a big effort. Then we move on to a final pull-up technique check. Some of the gym will be using big rubber bands to assist the pull up and some will be doing strictly body weight. It doesn't matter; we will ALL be pushing ourselves to our personal limit.

Eric yells, "go", and the room erupts into a frenzy of bodies hanging on bars and pulling themselves up as many times as they can. There are more bodies than bars, so those of us on the ground yell encouragement. Crossfit gets loud.

"Come on Katie, you can do it! One more, come on, just one more…pull…you've got it! Don't let up…. PULLLLLLL….YES!!!!" Everyone is cheering, it's a personal record for her and she's beaming as she writes it on the white board next to her name.

We all have friends and co-workers that we have known for a much longer time than our Crossfit friends but not people that we have bonded with so quickly. We all have people with whom we spend much more time, but we have precious few people in our lives with whom we have endured such pain and adversity. Most of us have even fewer people who have seen us physically collapse and who have admired us more for our courage and vulnerability.

And sadly most of us have too few people whose voices we have heard unfailingly over the noise of life, yelling our names, encouraging us to keep going. The Crossfit community is one of the most powerful examples of Tribe that I have ever witnessed.

GYM RAT

I've been an athlete my whole adult life. I ran cross-country in school, and competed in triathlons for 15 years before retiring to normal gym workouts to 'stay fit.' When I stopped competing as a triathlete I missed the camaraderie and the competition.

It didn't matter if the gym had great equipment and facilities, I would find myself getting bored and just going through the motions. I stayed somewhat fit, but I couldn't get myself to do the difficult functional workouts or to reach the intensity level I knew I needed on a consistent basis in order to achieve my real fitness goals.

I experimented with a number of different training patterns including personal training. The personal trainer was great; he gave me a specific plan and mixed up the workouts so my variety improved, but my travel schedule made it difficult to keep a normal rhythm in my trainer's calendar, and the lack of a compelling goal dulled my intensity.

Although I looked fit, my lack of core strength and other fitness attributes reared their ugly heads on a regular basis when I participated in the many outdoor activities I loved.

I thought, "This is ridiculous, I shouldn't be getting sore and hurt while skiing and playing golf!" I knew I needed to round out my fitness and incorporate intensity again, I just didn't know how.

Meanwhile in Santa Cruz, California, Greg Glassman was creating the answer to my fitness dreams and the dreams of hundreds of thousands of other people.

PURPOSE

Greg Glassman - a former gymnast and professional trainer - is not your typical gym trainer who makes a living leading people around a training circuit. He studies human performance, and he is experimenting and perfecting an entirely new way of looking at fitness.

Greg took serious issue with the word 'fitness'. Greg observed that there are really ten different facets that make up fitness. He found that specialized athletes became exceptionally *unfit* in many of those ten areas, so much so that they often failed even the simplest fitness tasks. Imagine a Kenyan marathoner trying to bench press!

In working with specialized athletes, Greg helped them to make tremendous improvements by 'rounding out' their fitness. He incorporated moves that had been neglected in order to improve performance in their core sport.

Greg observed that the same phenomenon with regular gym goers. Faithful gym rats were performing the same routines on the same isolation-based exercise machines, and, like their specialized professional athlete counterparts, they were woefully underdeveloped in a number of critical areas.

Greg isn't just concerned about professional athletes and gym rats, though. He is concerned about all of us. We all need to be able to perform basic functional movements well in order to lead a high quality of life, and to retain our independence.

If you think about it, the primary reason that anyone goes to a nursing home is an inability to stand up out of a chair and walk. As Greg will point out, this inability does not appear from old age, it appears from neglect and poor technique.

Greg Glassman was once asked;

"Can I enjoy optimal health without being an athlete?"

No!

Athletes experience a protection from the ravages of aging and disease that non-athletes never find. For instance, 80-year-old athletes are stronger than non-athletes in their prime at 25 years old. If you think that strength isn't important, consider that strength loss is what puts people in nursing homes. Athletes have greater bone density, stronger immune systems, less coronary heart disease, reduced cancer risk, fewer strokes, and less depression than non-athletes…The needs of an Olympic athlete and an 80 year old lady differ by degree, not kind.[v]

Greg is committed to redefining fitness not only for elite athletes, but for the population as a whole. His organization, Crossfit.com, is doing just that on a worldwide basis, at a rate untouched by any other gym franchise or workout regime in history.

REMARKABLE TERRITORY

Crossfit's specialty is NOT specializing… at least in terms of exercise; instead they focus on implementation and variety.

Greg believes that preparing for the diverse physical challenges of life is at odds with fixed, predictable, and routine regimens. Perhaps you don't consider the diversity of physical movement that you experience in a day; picking up heavy children, groceries, and occasionally furniture; Walking, climbing stairs, sitting and standing;

coaching your kids in sports, participating in sports like golf, cycling, or just playing in a neighborhood whiffle ball game.

> *"Train hard so you don't suck at life"*
> – Coach Greg Glassman

If you think about it, you can probably think back to an injury or two you suffered doing normal, everyday things. Greg sought to create a program that would prepare people for lifetime fitness and health, not just for what appears in the mirror. By asking the right question, Greg was able to look at all sport and physical tasks collectively, and ask, "What physical skills and adaptations would most universally lend themselves to performance advantage?"

Crossfit was born from studying and understanding all sports demands in order to prepare its participants for all of life's demands. In the end, Crossfit's specialty is NOT specializing… at least in terms of exercise; instead they focus on implementation.

You can trace Crossfit's success to the fact that its variable programming delivers results, but those results also come from the hard work and dedication of its participants. How does Crossfit succeed in getting its participants to do the work that regular gyms cannot?

The reason for its runaway success is that it harnesses intrinsic motivation like no other fitness program or philosophy. Greg and the Crossfit team developed an edge early on when they started to write actual times and other results on a white board at the gym.

In implementation, CrossFit is simply a sport—the "sport of fitness." We've learned that harnessing the natural camaraderie, competition, and fun of sport or game yields an intensity that cannot be matched by other means. The late Col. Jeff Cooper observed, "The fear of sporting failure is worse than the fear of death." It is our observation that men will die for points. By using whiteboards as scoreboards, keeping accurate scores and records, running a clock, and precisely defining the rules and standards for performance, we not only motivate unprecedented output but also derive both relative and absolute metrics at every workout; this data has important value well beyond motivation.[vi]

FUNDING MECHANISM

Think about Greg's purpose. He wants to redefine fitness for everyone, so he needs a mechanism to put the opportunity in front of the world. He needs people to stick with it, get results and recruit others. That's a tall order.

Consider that Gold's Gym, previously the world's largest fitness center operator, has about 800 locations worldwide that have been created since its founding in 1965.

Crossfit is only 10 years old and has over 6,500 gym locations worldwide and still growing rapidly. How is that possible?

The answer is open source. Coach Glassman provided a construct for trainers worldwide to create their own gyms. The cost of entry for a Crossfit gym affiliation is as follows: a $1,000 weekend certification course; an application; an essay demonstrating that you're doing this from your heart; and a $3,000 yearly affiliation fee. Because of the simplicity of Crossfit's training regimen, you can equip a very nice gym for under $25,000, and many are achieved for far less.

The open source model of Crossfit has made the dream of gym ownership a reality for thousands of trainers worldwide. They, in turn, are making the dream of elite fitness accessible to their communities.

EMPLOYEE MANAGEMENT

The application essay is a key part of the Crossfit franchise. It's a method of controlling who joins the tribe, and that they are going to carry the Crossfit brand and mission forward. The reality is that because of its open source design, Crossfit is not for every trainer. Trainers looking for a formula, corporate marketing materials, franchise rules, etc., simply won't make it.

Opening a successful Crossfit box requires entrepreneurship because the website, the equipment, the setup, the marketing, the membership sales, the staffing, the programming; they're all up to you.

As a result, Crossfit attracts exactly the DNA they seek which means that Crossfit HQ can forgo a whole host of functions that their franchise gym counterparts cannot. Crossfit HQ is a simple organism. No VP's of this or that, and lots of independent contractors.

CUSTOMER MANAGEMENT

Crossfit's reputation is built upon results, which are built upon effort, which is built upon tribal support. If the tribe gets 'sick', Crossfit will cease to be Crossfit.

Once again, it turns out that the best controls do not come from management; they come from ever present, persistent natural forces of human behavior. In the case of Crossfit, that force is the need for the Tribe to protect the Tribe.

The Crossfit tribe knows that their enjoyment and their success can never be independent from the peers in their group. For the system to work, the tribe needs to support AND hold each other accountable. They must miss and be missed.

Membership sales at Crossfit belong mostly to the tribe. The majority of new members come from referrals and in many cases outright sales activity of its existing members.

Once in the door, prospects go through an orientation that exposes them to exercises and equipment that will most likely be very new to them. They get a taste of their first efforts against the clock.

Members that get through the filters of the tribe and orientation generally stick with the program and quickly become a part of the merry Crossfit gang.

EVERYTHING YOU NEED IS IN THE BOX

Crossfit's growth rate is remarkable because it is the antithesis of most exercise and weight loss programs. It is not easy, it is time-consuming and it's not cheap. That, in and of itself, is a clue that there is something special going on.

Crossfit provides the tribal nutrients that we all crave:

> **Autonomy**, the gym owner can establish any theme they like. There is Crossfit Southie located in Boston's historically Irish south end decorated in shamrocks, there's Crossfit Farenheit in Dubai, and even Crossfit Golf.

Mastery, Crossfit is 1/3 gymnastics, 1/3 Olympic weight lifting, and 1/3 cardio conditioning. The program employs so many moves and combinations of moves that you can spend a lifetime pursuing mastery of a broad and inclusive fitness.

Belonging; Crossfit is as much about the shared experience as it is about the actual physical work. When you become a part of a Crossfit gym, you are welcomed into a family of people with whom you share a common interest in exceptional health. The cause you share is important because it affects all of our lives to such a great degree.

> *"The world breaks everyone, and afterward, some are strong at the broken places."*
> - Ernest Hemingway

Crossfit is helping a lot of people get stronger mentally, physically, emotionally, and spiritually. When you infuse your business with meaning like that you reap unparalleled powers of growth and resilience. You also impact engagement.

And you also impact the world.

ONE
YOUR REMARKABLE MISSION

SERVICE DESIGN

Too many companies think that service excellence is being all things to all customers and trying to match the competition. Pursuing this view of excellence is a guarantee that you will end up delivering average products for average people (in the remarkable economy average people are becoming extinct). This approach is an exercise in futility and a race to the bottom of your market.

Doc Franson is ok saying goodbye to a patient that isn't committed to their own wellness. Coach Glassman isn't trying to please the drive by gym masses that want to vegetate on some cardio equipment with headphones.

This kind of focus takes discipline and it takes coordination, and it takes a commitment to make sure that the hill you claim to excel at is truly remarkable. The easiest way to be consistent and focused is to work on something that is aligned with your personal intention.

INSPIRATION

The inspiration that you provide as a leader makes your organization a more human place for your team. But it's also the most powerful marketing strategy there is just so long as you do these two things;

1. R*eally* stand for what you say you stand for.

2. Align what your offer with your intention and vice versa.

> *"Our principles are our procedures and our procedures are our principles"*
> CJ MERTZ

VALUE

I can't say enough about the power of engagement. Your team needs the same thing that you do; a regular opportunity to grow, explore and master something. We all want to be great in some way. We all want to feel a sense of pride that our efforts are building personal equity of some kind.

The notion that some people are just meant to do meaningless work is flat wrong. Your work environment may literally be a factory floor, but that doesn't mean that the job has to be brainless and soulless.

TRIBAL MECHANISM

Each of the four remarkable story example companies leverage at least one tribal mechanism. Remember, here is what people are looking for in a tribe;

1. To **belong** to a group

2. To be **inspired** by the group's cause

3. To become **valued** as a member of the group

And the mechanism looks like this;

1. Members connected to a leader's cause

2. Leader communicating with members

3. Members communicating with members

4. Members communicating back to their leader

I think that this is the most fun and creative aspect of remarkability. There are an infinite number of ways to link your tribe together. There is no right way, just your way. As long as the mechanism works, you're good. We're going to talk about where and how to begin in just a minute, but first I want to make sure that you're properly riled up.

A REMARKABLE RANT

The factory mentality brought us unprecedented access to life changing conveniences. It allowed developed countries to redefine quality of life generation after generation.

For the first time in history, our youngest generation is expected to have a *lower* standard of living AND a lower life expectancy than their parents. Paradoxically, our quest for convenience has morphed into a quest for stuff that fails to give us the meaning, connection and growth we so desperately crave.

> *For the first time in history, our youngest generation is expected to have a lower standard of living AND a lower life expectancy than their parents.*

If stuff could make us happy we would be REALLY happy, but 75% of our workforce could use a heck of a lot more meaning in their lives.

I, along with many of my business friends, have been 'screaming' for political leadership to step up and defend the business environment. "Don't let health care costs, financial regulation and taxes prevent us from being able to reinvest, create new jobs and compete!" we all cry.

But the more I observe the discussion, the media coverage and the political maneuvering the more I have come to realize that my cries - our cries - are resembling the classic definition of insanity – doing the same thing over and over again and expecting a different result.

Don't get me wrong, the selection of our political leadership is vital, but we have to get real. Our government is a reflection of us as a society. Rather than take responsibility for our own choices, we have over-spent and over-eaten to avoid reality. We have become addicted to short term fixes, Band-Aids and pills. We have treated symptoms rather than addressing root causes. Our government is merely a reflection of our own behavior.

Ironically, people who are tired of being manipulated with carrots and sticks are rallying to elect leaders whose primary tool IS carrots and sticks….disguised as new laws, regulations and programs.

These people expect their elected officials to *lead* them somewhere better, to give them something bigger to believe in. But we haven't elected 'true' leaders; we have elected self-servants to tell us what we want to hear and to enable our dysfunctional behavior.

Our leaders are following OUR cues! We demonstrate through our behavior that it's ok to over indulge and manipulate because we practice it in every aspect of our personal and professional lives.

Expecting politicians to behave better than we do is not realistic. Do as I say, not as a do, is not an effective way to lead.

This is a stand off!

We don't have money deficits and fat surpluses. We have a leadership deficit and a victim surplus.

We're behaving 'badly' as a society because we are lost in transition between an economic-management model that served us extremely well, until it didn't, and a new emerging model that is not widely understood. Our entire economic problem is the aggregate result of millions of troubled micro economies.

You and I, and our many entrepreneurial-minded friends, are the leaders of our own micro cultures. It is up to us to lead from the ground up and create a tipping point in which true, inspired leadership becomes the norm over bureaucratic management. It is up to us to restore engagement and repair quality of life within our micro cultures, and in turn improve the standard of living in the communities we serve.

The people you influence directly and indirectly need just four simple things. The great news is that you can provide them for FREE. And doing so will increase *your* level of engagement, your legacy, and your **BOTTOM LINE.**

1. A game they feel they can win.

2. A big reason to believe

3. A place to belong

4. An important role to play

I was once told that the more influence you have, the more responsibility you have. YOU have influence, you have a responsibility, AND you have an opportunity. Any way you choose to look at it, pursuing remarkability is your calling and it is a benefit. A HUGE benefit.

Don't wait for the political 'leadership' to create the world you wished you lived in, use your entrepreneurial power to do what you do best, CREATE it!

REMARKABLE ACTION

Some of you own your own businesses and some of you are leaders within businesses. Each of you has already developed aspects of the big four needs already. The key to taking it to the next level is to more deliberately incorporate the big four in your strategy and to lead based on the big four. You likely already have everything you need to do it.

To begin, RIGHT NOW before you forget the commitment you feel right now, go to the link below

1. Go to www.remarkablebook.com to learn how you use Remarkable Market Force to catapult you and your business to the next level.

2. Give copies of this book to your team and plan a discussion around it aimed at incorporating this method in your strategic planning process.

3. Then pass your copy of this book on to a fellow business leader to spread the idea of rendering our world remarkable through an epidemic of remarkable companies.

Never forget that you and your team have vast untapped energy and creativity, capable of solving 'unsolvable' problems. And solving 'unsolvable problems' is the stuff that makes remarkable stories.

You've waited long enough, now is *your* time. Go for it.

ENDNOTES

i. Dan Pink, Drive (New York, Riverhead Books, 2009), 59

ii. Aesch, *Driving Excellence* (New York: Hyperion, 2011), 1

iii. Aesch, *Driving Excellence* (New York: Hyperion, 2011), 84

iv. Aesch, *Driving Excellence* (New York: Hyperion, 2011), 42-43

v. Greg Glassman, *Crossfit Training Guide, 8*

vi. Greg Glassman, *Crossfit Training Guide, 4*

CPSIA information can be obtained at www.ICGtesting.com
Printed in the USA
LVOW01s1907160314

377630LV00015B/1294/P

9 781629 213477